SHOWERS OF

PENTECOST

'A TREASURY OF TESTIMONIES'

PEARL SPENCER (NÉE HAWKINS)

Edited/Compiled by BEN ALLSOP

To the memory of Pearl, her parents – Walter (Jnr.) and Hilda – and her grandparents, Walter (Snr.) and Charlotte ('Lottie') Hawkins and William and Florence ('Florrie') Potter.

"For ... after (they) had served (their) own generation by the will of God, (they) fell asleep.'

(Acts 13:36, NKJV[1])

---

[1] Unless specified otherwise, all Scripture quotations in this book will be taken from the *New King James Version* (NKJV).

CONTENTS

Foreword: MICK SPENCER
Commendation: PROF. WILLIAM K. KAY
Preface: BEN ALLSOP

Postscript: BEN ALLSOP

Foreword: MICK SPENCER

I first met Pearl the week before Christmas 1987; at the time, she was working for the Avon cosmetics company as a sales agent. Pearl was supplying the girlfriend of my brother, Geoff, with beauty products. During this meeting, Pearl invited Geoff and his girlfriend to a Christmas concert at her church. Geoff swiftly declined but volunteered me to take his place, instead!

Attending that concert was to prove the night I made the life-transforming decision to follow Jesus Christ.

From the moment I met Pearl, I was aware of a commitment to her faith that I had not noted in any believer before. Both Pearl and I had experienced failed marriages and a later relationship in Pearl's life had bought her to a place of deep repentance and a love for her Saviour which was very clear and very powerful. Within days of our first meeting, we mutually committed to spending the rest of our lives together and we married several months later. Her zeal for the Lord never faulted during our years together and I was grafted into a family where Jesus Christ was the central figure. You will read more about Pearl's parents and grandparents in this book – all of whom made significant contributions to the Pentecostal movement and advancement of the gospel in this nation and abroad, especially in the Congo.

Through the years, I heard many stories and accounts from Pearl and her parents – Walter and Hilda - of miraculous events, healings and divine encounters. Around a decade into our marriage, Pearl started to record these stories and compile them in her free time and or when she felt the urge to write. Unfortunately, a busy life curtailed the full completion of many stories but hopefully you will go on to read and be inspired by the testimonies included in this book which our brother, Ben, kindly afforded his time to progress and complete to this point. I trust that the details in these stories are truthful and accurate as Pearl was meticulous with detail.

At the time of writing this Forward, it is a little less than three years since Pearl's passing (her parents, Walter and Hilda, having passed previously in 2015 and 2011, respectively). I have been in some pretty dark, emotional places in the past months - so knowing Pearl's work is finally being realised is a joy and also a part of my own healing journey.

May you be encouraged reading this book as we look forward to the fact that Jesus Christ Himself will soon be calling all of His loved ones home and 'we shall all be changed – in a moment, in the twinkling of an eye, at the last trumpet.'[2] Maranatha[3] – come, Lord Jesus!

Mick Spencer

May 2024

---

[2] 1 Corinthians 15:52
[3] 1 Corinthians 16:22. Consists of two Aramean words, Maran'athah, meaning, 'our Lord comes' or 'is coming'.

Commendation:
PROF. WILLIAM K. KAY

The outpouring of the Holy Spirit in Britain started before the First World War and was initially shaped by the Sunderland conventions which ran from 1908 until the war started in 1914. In January 1909, the first Pentecostal missionary organisation was set up, the Pentecostal Missionary Union (PMU), by two Anglicans, the Rev. Alexander Boddy and Cecil Polhill. Consequently, Pentecostal mission overseas began very early – even before the Pentecostal denominations had been established - and, because Polhill himself had been a missionary in China, that was the main field targeted. Missionaries, it was soon realised, needed training before they launched themselves overseas to an uncertain but faith-filled future. Therefore, the first Pentecostal training school was set up at almost the same time as the PMU and one of those who attended the school in Preston was W. F. P. Burton (1886-1971).

Whilst George Jeffreys, another graduate of the school, campaigned in Northern Ireland and founded the Elim Evangelistic Band in 1915, Burton sailed out to the Congo to begin his vast missionary endeavours. Jeffreys, together with his brother Stephen and his nephew Edward, campaigned vigorously in Britain and made a huge impact in the interwar years before 1939. Crusades were organised, the gospel was preached, large crowds attended, many people were healed, and Pentecostalism in Britain was launched in a blaze of miracles and enough publicity to generate reports in the Christian press as well as the secular newspapers. The book you are about to read tells you, amongst other things, how the ministry of the Jeffreys brothers was personally felt by one particular family.

But, whilst the war was being fought in Europe, Burton and his companions reached Mwanza, Congo. It is an understatement to say that the situation was tough for them. One of Burton's companions turned back and then another died as the boat carrying them motored upriver but Burton and Salter pressed on and eventually over more than 40 years made huge inroads into the Congo and set up congregations in many scattered villages. One of those who went out to serve in the mission founded by Burton and Salter was Walter Hawkins who later became an important member of the Overseas Missions Council in British Assemblies of God. All those missionaries who had gone out with the Pentecostal Missionary Union were absorbed into British Assemblies of God when it was formed in 1924. This was a deliberate and strategic amalgamation because it placed responsibility on the new Pentecostal assemblies in the United Kingdom to fund and support the overseas missionaries. The Assemblies of God missionary council coordinated and provided a central home base and point of contact for the missionaries and Walter Hawkins became a key man in this organisational network because, after his service on the field in

Congo was over, he was elected to serve in the AoG offices in Britain from 1963 till his retirement in 1979. He was ideally placed to do so because he had experience on the mission field whilst also being an able administrator.

In this book you will read not only about events in the Congo retold from personal experience but also accounts of healings and divine guidance within a circle of friends and family. This is what early Pentecostalism was like. Miracles were reported by ordinary people and, in these pages, we re-live the surprise and joy these healings brought and the closeness to Jesus that was fostered. Miracles at home built faith for mission abroad. In those days, before commercial air travel or face-to-face digital communication across the globe, to go as a missionary was to close the door (perhaps forever) on the familiar British town or village where you had grown up and with courage to venture into a hard life in a distant land because you loved and trusted Jesus. You needed to be sure. You needed to be prepared spiritually through prayer and sometimes by dreams and visions. And when you arrived, you found difficulties you had to overcome. We glimpse these realities and start to feel and imagine the cost of missionary discipleship.

If you want to read more about the Congo Evangelistic Mission, I recommend:

Harold Womersley (1973), *Wm F. P. Burton: Congo Pioneer*, Eastbourne, Victory Press. More expensive and more academic is David Emmett (2021), *W.F.P. Burton (1886-1971): A Pentecostal Pioneer's Missional Vision for Congo*, Leiden, Brill.

Insights into Burton's early years are given in the papers below which you may be able to access online:

Garrard, D. J. (2012). Burton's Early Years of Ministry and Doctrine under the auspices of the PMU. *Journal of the European Pentecostal Theological Association, 32*(1), 3–14.
https://doi.org/10.1179/jep.2012.32.1.002
Garrard, D. J. (2012). W. F. P. Burton and his Missionary Call. *Journal of the European Pentecostal Theological Association, 32*(2), 237–248.
https://doi.org/10.1179/jep.2012.32.2.009

Garrard, D. J. (2013). William F.P. Burton and the Rupture with the PMU. *Journal of the European Pentecostal Theological Association, 33*(1), 14–27.
https://doi.org/10.1179/jep.2013.33.1.003

If you want to know more about the ministry of the Jeffreys brothers, then:
Desmond Cartwright (1986), *The Great Evangelists*, Basingstoke, Marshall Pickering.

A full account of the life of George Jeffreys is given in:

William K. Kay (2017), *George Jeffreys: Pentecostal Apostle and Revivalist*, Cleveland, TN, CPT Press.

The story of Edward Jeffreys is told by:

David Watts (with Geoffrey Green and Robert Mountford) (2017), *Edward Jeffreys: Healing evangelist, his story, movement and legacy*, Stourbridge, Transformations Publications.

Prof. William K Kay

June 2024

Preface: BEN ALLSOP

'We will not hide these truths from our children; we will tell the next generation about the glorious deeds of the LORD, about His power and His mighty wonders.' PSALM 78:4, NLT

From the onset of my conversion to Christ, I have been fascinated by the heritage of Pentecostal Christianity in my family. I am a fourth generation Pentecostal; our 'family pioneer' being my great-grandmother, Doris Roe (1912-1996). Hitherto a Methodist, 'Nana Roe' (*as I refer to her*) suffered some ostracisation in her local community when she switched allegiances in 1949 to the Pentecostals, who met at North Wingfield Assembly of God. Nana Roe went on to be a trailblazer for Jesus in the Derbyshire village of Grassmoor where she lived, pointing many to her beloved Saviour through her Christ-like example.

Her eldest daughter (my Nana), Sylvia G. Dawes (1934-2015) would regale me with stories of growing up at North Wingfield Assembly – being baptised by full immersion there as a teenager and receiving the baptism of the Holy Spirit unexpectedly in her bedroom, feeling 'guilty' as she had planned to go to the 'Tarrying Meeting' that night … but received her own Pentecost, a few hours 'ahead of schedule'! She spoke affectionately of the Hawkins and Colliss families, who were so instrumental in leading the church in those days. Thus, these names and their stories were imprinted in my mind from a young age – and I came to appreciate the providential roles these dear saints played in the 'grace narrative' God has been writing in my family, over the generations.

Let us fast forward to 2022 … the 3rd of July, to be precise. It was a Sunday and my wife (Elisha) and I were visiting the Holmewood Assembly (Abundant Life Christian Centre, ALCC) to hear our friend, Peter Cavanna, minister as guest preacher. As Peter took to the pulpit, he didn't rush into his prepared message; instead, a prophetic anointing descended upon him. The man of God approached me on the front row, laid his hand upon me and an inspired utterance proceeded from his lips:

'There is coming a turning of the page for you!

A real turning is coming … you thought a few pages would turn but there are some pages to turn yet.

Imagine a favourite Uncle showing you a box that he will leave you. He shows you things that are in the box … they're so dear to him … of no financial value, but precious.

You're going to inherit soon! Some 'old things' that need to stay around, even after the 'old ones' have gone.

Take the bones of Joseph on to the next stage.

You're going to inherit a responsibility … an anointing … an 'old fire'.

Have a look in the box … all of this is going to belong to you. You will have to take care of it. You will have to cherish it.

Why? Because the LORD knows that you understand the value of it. It won't be given to others ... they won't know its value. They'll throw it away.

Now is not the day to inherit ... but that day is coming soon!

May an 'old fashioned flame' continue to be upon your life.

In my sixteen years of involvement in charismatic Christianity (to date), this has proved to be my most significant and life-changing experience of prophetic ministry. There was a 'holy hush' in the congregation and a witness in the spirits of those present that the Lord had truly spoken. It went unsaid at the time: but I knew – and the existing leadership at ALCC knew – that the Lord was calling me to '*inherit a responsibility*' there. The prophecy said '*now is not the day to inherit*' ... so we '*kept all these things, and pondered them in (our) heart(s)*'[4] ...and waited for the '*fullness of the time*'[5].

Without forcing things, it came to pass the following year that our Assembly - Lifehouse Church (formerly 'Zion'), Chesterfield – released us to ALCC in the autumn. Now as Associate Leader of ALCC, the Lord has called me to '*take the bones of Joseph*' forward into a new era and at the time of writing (May 2024), we are seeing growth, wonderful answers to prayer and an increased expectation in the weekly meetings. For this, we give God all the glory and believe that 'the best is yet to come'!

---

[4] Luke 2:19
[5] Galatians 4:4

In Scripture, prophecy often has a long-term and short-term fulfilment; for example, in Jesus' Olivet Discourse[6], He described the impending destruction of Jerusalem in 70AD and the eschatological signs of the end of age together, such that it is unclear where one prophecy begins and another ends. In my understanding, taking on the Associate Leader role at ALCC is the 'long-term fulfilment' of the prophecy, given by Peter Cavanna to myself. However – before this – I received a 'down-payment' of the prophecy through a remarkable connection with Mick Spencer.

As an enthusiast of Pentecostal history, I am a member of the Facebook group 'Yesterday' – where people associated with the Assemblies of God share photos and reminisce of days gone by. Mick Spencer – whom I did not know – posted a picture from his late wife's archives, featuring Congo missionaries Willie Burton, Teddy Hodgson, Harold Womersley and others. His late wife was Pearl, only child of Walter (Jnr.) and Hilda Hawkins. Of course, I knew of the Hawkins family from my own family connections. My Nana's younger sister, Susan (of similar age to Pearl) had told me how she was at Grassmoor Infant School with her when the Hawkins family were on furlough from the Congo. Walter – something of a village celebrity as 'The Congo Missionary' – would come into the school by invitation and enthral the young scholars with exciting slides from the African continent. I was saddened to hear that Pearl

---

[6] Matthew 24, Mark 13, Luke 21

had passed away from ovarian cancer in September 2021 and I relayed this sad news to her former school mate, my 'Auntie Sue'.

I initiated an online conversation with Mick via Facebook Messenger which resulted in him inviting me over to the home that he and Pearl had shared, not too far away from where my wife and I live in Clowne, Derbyshire. Mick and I spoke of Pearl over cups of tea … of her parents and grandparents … of her upbringing on the mission field and a plethora of other related subjects. As a recently widowed man, Mick evidently ached for Pearl – but he was trying to keep a 'practical head' and clear out some possessions that had belonged to Pearl and her family. Amongst these were some rare, early British Pentecostal literature that had belonged to her Dad and Grandad – including her Grandad's well-worn Bible. Mick knew I was very much invested in the history of the family and knew that I would appreciate being the recipient of such precious items: so they were given to me! It was quite something to imagine that the very Bible my Nana will have heard Walter Hawkins (Snr.) preach from back in the '30s/'40s/50s … was now in the possession of her grandson, all these decades later!

In addition to the books and photos that Mick handed over, he made me aware that Pearl had been writing a book: recording testimonies of God's miraculous working in the life of her family and those she has known, over the course of her life. Apparently, Pearly began writing in the late 1990s and wrote chapters here and there, as and when she had the time between working-full time, being a wife and mother and looking after her then elderly parents.

The book remained unpublished – saved on a memory device, each chapter on a different file. Some chapters were complete; others only 'half-done'. Mick sent me the files as email attachments, authorising me to make use of the writings as I saw fit. He acknowledged that – in his grief – he felt unable to move forward with Pearl's writings; however, he felt that some of these recollections would be of significant worth to the Pentecostal movement, with some of the stories pre-dating even the founding of the Assemblies of God itself.

So … here we have another fulfilment of the prophecy … inheriting *'some 'old things' that need to stay around, even after the 'old ones' have gone.'* I did not go searching for these things – the books, the photos, the unfinished work of Pearl Spencer. They have been left to me as per the prophecy … to be a custodian of. Quite honestly: they might have passed into hands that may not have appreciated the worth of such things.

'You will have to take care of it. You will have to cherish it. Why? Because the LORD knows that you understand the value of it.'

Again, we fast-forward to May 2024. It's half term and both myself and Elisha are 'on leave', given we are both secondary school teachers. Amidst the busyness of life, I was reminded of the email attachments Mick had sent me, some time before.

I opened them again … read through some … and knew that I *had* to do something. I could not let such *'praiseworthy deeds of the LORD'* as recounted in Pearl's writings go unremembered. Indeed, the twenty-first century Pentecostal church – birthed in revival scenes – needs to be reminded of how it began, that we might hunger and thirst for God to move mightily again *in our generation*, by His Spirit!

I began to download the files … put the chapters together … and read through. I was captivated and read pretty much solidly, well into the early hours of the following day. Essentially, the book was 'already there'. Only infrequently did I have to make minor amendments. In some instances, a story was only 'half baked'; evidently, Pearl intended on asking her parents for further details of an anecdote but unfortunately, never got around to it. In these instances, the half-finished story was deleted. However, the vast majority of the chapters were finished to a very high standard and can be read here, just as Pearl intended them to be read. Pearl did not produce a *Contents* page … Mick believes that she would have done this, upon the book's completion… so I have had to order the chapters myself. Fortunately, each chapter is quite distinct and a linear narrative (in terms of timeline) has not been necessary; thus, the ordering of chapters is quite inconsequential. Nevertheless, I have endeavoured to put the more 'significant' chapters towards the front of the work; some of the later chapters end quite abruptly as they were unfinished but have sufficient 'gold' in them for them to still be included in the work.

So … with Mick's backing … I ensured that Pearl's book finally got published, spurred on by the encouragement of friends/contacts in AoG circles such as Peter Cavanna, Dr. Steven Jenkins and Prof. William K. Kay. I am particularly grateful to Prof. Kay for providing a *Commendation*: a tremendous honour for such a scholarly man to endorse an unscholarly – but I trust *important* – book! Thank you to Dr. Jenkins for sharing his wealth of experience with regards to self-publishing with *Amazon*: it did prove to be a relatively painless process, after all! I also extend my gratitude to Laura Murray of *Peanut Designs* (also co-pastor of *His Kingdom Church*, Hull) for the excellent book cover.

Pearl's work was untitled and so I set about finding a suitable Pentecostal 'name' for the book. I quickly discovered from a browse of the Internet that many Pentecostal phrases have already been used as book titles …but the term '*Showers of Pentecost*' had hitherto gone unclaimed! I derived the phrase from the verse of a Charles Wesley hymn, found in the beloved *Redemption Hymnal*[7], as below:

> '*Lord, we believe to us and ours,*
>
> *The Apostolic promise given;*
>
> *We wait the Pentecostal showers,*
>
> *The Holy Ghost send down from heaven.*'

My heart's cry is: *Yes, Lord! Revive Your work in our day, O God"!*

---

[7] Hymn 234, Assemblies of God Publishing House, London

My humble prayer is that the '*God who answers by fire*'[8] will take this collection of writings written by Pearl Spencer and use them to inspire a new generation to lay hold of God by faith and see the Kingdom of God push back the darkness, both near and afar.

Amen!

Ben Allsop

Associate Leader, Abundant Life Christian Centre (Holmewood)

May 2024

---

[8] 1 Kings 18:24

CHAPTER 1:

The Jeffreys Phenomenon

'Divine healing is the gift of God to the sufferer in need.' ANNE WHITE[9]

Miraculous signs and wonders spearhead every significant move of God on planet Earth. In each new dispensation, God raises up extraordinary people who have a fresh revelation of the eternal purposes of God; people who are God's messengers to their generation, who understand the ethos of their time, the needs of their fellow men, and who are willing to sacrifice all for God's cause.

Stephen and George Jeffreys were God's gifting to the British Isles in the first part of the 20th century and from Britain to the world through those who caught their vision. They began as simple miners from Aberaman in South Wales but God touched this family in a singular way with a powerful anointing to preach the good news of Jesus Christ and to pray for the sick to be healed.

My father, Walter Hawkins, was amongst those fired up by their zeal for God. As a boy and young man, he met each of them

---

[9] Anne White was blessed with a healing ministry for the emotionally sick and disturbed and wrote the best seller "Healing Adventure". An American Episcopalian lay-woman, she was a popular speaker at charismatic conferences, camps and other Christian gatherings in Japan, Sweden, Norway, England and all over the USA.

personally, heard their gospel messages, saw the astonishing miracles of healing in their meetings and was inspired by their love and passion for the lost, the suffering and the damaged souls of humanity.

The youngest Jeffrey brother, George, became the founder and 'Principal' of the Elim Foursquare Gospel Alliance. In his book *'In Defence of His Word'*[10], Robert Ernest Darragh wrote that, as George preached his compelling message that the Bible promises healing for the body as well as salvation for the soul, '— *faces were lit up with hope.*' Until then, God's gifts of healing had been more or less resigned to history. Darragh describes how one morning George stood at the crossroads of his life *'... at the end of one road a voice called him over the sea to the great continent of America, and response would mean no financial worry, but a life of ease and personal comfort; ... at the end of the other road a voice called from Ireland, and he knew it was the voice of God. Nothing was promised except a hard-uphill fight and difficulties that only God could take one through ...and so one morning a lonely figure stepped onto Irish soil with his message.'*

17 years later, after much hardship and persecution for his beliefs, George Jeffreys was able to assert, *'I will not cease to declare the whole counsel of God.'* Thus, it was he - amongst others -who raised a standard for those who preach the full 'Foursquare'

---

[10] First published by Elim Publishing Company Ltd., London in Sept 1932. Darragh was one of the first members of the Elim Evangelistic Band in 1915.

Gospel of Jesus Christ: that He is the 'Saviour, Healer, Baptiser and Coming King'.[11]

Probably the most widely acclaimed of the brothers was Stephen Jeffreys who was fondly known by his generation as "The Beloved Evangelist". His ministry spanned several continents and he was truly a forerunner of the contemporary world evangelist. Yet just as Jesus completed His public ministry in 3 short years, so Stephen Jeffreys achieved the bulk of his remarkable effort for God in only 7 years, with hundreds of thousands reached with the gospel message and many thousands visibly healed of sickness.

Another brother, William Jeffreys, also had a miraculous ministry similar to George and Stephen, though he was less well known. He joined the Assemblies of God movement along with Stephen, whilst George became the founder of the Elim Churches, as previously alluded to. Often Stephen would spearhead a campaign and then William would follow on to establish the work, as happened in Doncaster in May 1928. In September that year, over 100 converts were baptised in the local Baptist Church by Pastor W.J. Thomas, with a further 119 the following year, thus creating a sizeable congregation.

Edward Jeffreys, son of Stephen, is lesser known today, possibly because he concentrated his efforts around the Stoke area in The Potteries of England. Yet those who witnessed his powerful

---

[11] A concept attributed to Aimee Semple McPherson (1890-1944), founder of The Foursquare Church denomination.

meetings and the phenomenal healing miracles that took place affirm that more people were healed by God during Edward's ministry than through his illustrious father and uncles' country-wide and even world-wide crusades.

George Jeffreys

This is the tribute paid by Donald Gee, a founding member of the British Assemblies of God and a great family friend. Whenever Donald Gee stayed at our house for the monthly Overseas Missions board meetings, he would insist on sampling Mum's baking, especially her "melting moments" and "coffee kisses" – he was certainly a man of great discernment!

DONALD GEE: *'We salute George Jeffreys as one of our great pioneers and a notable gift of Christ to His Church.'* [12]

'George Jeffreys was easily the most gifted preacher that the British Pentecostal Movement has produced. He had a voice like music, with sufficient Welsh intonation to add an inimitable charm. His platform personality at times was magnetic; his face was appealing and although lacking academic training he possessed a natural refinement that made him acceptable in all circles. He

---

[12] From his personal memoirs "These Men I Knew", Assemblies of God Publishing House, 1980.

presented his message with a logical appeal and a note of authority that was compelling.'

'As a promising young Welsh evangelist, George Jeffreys began to conduct small campaigns with increasing success. An invitation in 1915 to hold a mission in Monaghan in Northern Ireland marked an important step forward and it was there that he began to gather round him a band of men whose hearts God had touched, chief of whom was Ernest Darragh who became his faithful lifelong friend and campaign manager. They took the name of the "Elim Evangelistic Band".' [13]

'At first their pioneering work was exclusively in Ireland with headquarters in Belfast; but the hunger in the mainland Pentecostal groups to see something moving in Home Evangelism led to pressing invitations to cross the sea. Early campaigns were successful and finally in 1922 the Headquarters of the Elim Movement were moved to Clapham in S.W. London where they acquired an old nunnery standing in four acres of ground, which they named "Elim Woodlands". This housed the Elim Bible College and other properties were added for offices.'

'George Jeffrey's rise to fame became almost meteoric through his evangelistic and divine healing campaigns that soon filled the largest public halls in the country. A high point was achieved in

---

[13] Another member of the group in Northern Ireland was John Carter who later became the General Secretary of the British Assemblies of God, working alongside my father Walter Hawkins in the AoG Offices and who later served with him on the Overseas Missions Council.

1926 when Elim pioneered their first Easter Convention in the Royal Albert Hall in London. This was followed by great gatherings in the Crystal Palace and scores of Elim churches were opened as a result.'

'At the Great European Pentecostal Conference in Stockholm in 1939 I drove with George Jeffreys and Lewi Pethrus to the large marquee outside the city where the evening meetings were held. Jeffreys preached superbly through an interpreter and this was a high-water mark of his life. Pethrus was thrilled and admired him ever after.'

'Soon after this in 1940 George Jeffreys left the Elim movement he had founded with such blessing and formed a small group called the "Bible Pattern Church Fellowship." After that his health began to fail and gradually he ceased to be in the public eye. He died in January 1962 at the age of 72 and his funeral drew a large congregation to the Kensington Temple.'

'In spite of the clouds that dimmed the evening glory of his years, George Jeffreys remains a stirring memory as one of the outstanding evangelists of the first half of the 20th Century. His ministry could truly be described as that of an apostle for he not only won thousands of converts and healed the sick but he established many churches that stand to this day.'

My father, Walter Hawkins, has a very special recollection of a George Jeffrey's crusade meeting that galvanised his faith in the miraculous power of God:

WALTER: *'It was like the Lord Jesus gathering people on earth and healing all who came.'*

'I was only 12 years old when I first heard George Jeffreys preach. It was the summer of 1930 and Mam, Dad and I were spending a couple of weeks during the school holidays with my Aunt Min and Uncle Dick at Greenough House in Bonsall. By then I was extremely interested in a young lass called Hilda who lived next door at Chestnuts Farm – she later became my wife, of course. That year I had begun to grow at last and to my relief she was no longer towering over me!'

'Mam and Dad had already heard that the great healing evangelist George Jeffreys was coming in July to preach for a fortnight in Birmingham, so they arranged to take a small group from Bonsall to one of the midweek afternoon meetings. My heart leapt in anticipation, not only at the chance to see this famous preacher and possibly witness some remarkable miracles first hand, but also I was secretly hoping that my young sweetheart Hilda would be coming along, too! Since our family home was miles away in Grassmoor, the only opportunity I had to see her during each year was at an occasional convention meeting or when my mother was invited to preach in the Bonsall Assembly, and even then we could only share a stolen glance or two, our blushes displaying for all to see our keen interest in each other.'

'I could hardly wait for the special day to arrive. We all had an early lunch and then Mr. Dunkerley (the Bonsall taxi driver) pulled up outside Aunt Min's at about 12.30pm.'

'Up at the farm, Hilda had been waiting as expectantly as I had for a chance to see the great preacher. "Mam," she cried. "Can I go, too? Please, Mam, please!!"'

'"There's no room, lass," Florrie replied sadly, disappointed herself as she witnessed the portly frames of Aunt Min and Mrs Sheldon disappearing into the small minibus down the lane along with the Hawkins family and one or two others.'

'Hilda hung her head in abject disappointment. Tied to the farm work, her father William Potter had no possibility of leaving his animals for a day's outing to Birmingham, no matter how important it was, and even her 16-year-old brother Oswald had been denied a coveted seat next to me, his pal Walter, in the minibus.'

'So it was that, squeezed in the back seat between two sweaty bodies, I sadly waved my distant sweetheart goodbye. Still, I could not stay disappointed for long. The George Jeffreys Campaign in Birmingham was a great event for the budding Pentecostal movement and hundreds of cars and minibuses were converging on the Bingley Exhibition Hall from all directions. You could feel the excitement growing as crowds gathered from every corner of Britain.'

'"*Imagine Bingley Hall crammed with seats and every seat occupied*," reported the Birmingham Gazette, June 5th 1930.

"Imagine the galleries crowded and people wedged tight in, and doors left open to let in the air."

'Our party managed to find seats just to the right of the long central aisle, about one third of the way back. I was so pleased that we could get a good view of proceedings. Then the meeting started and we all stood as George Jeffreys walked onto the stage – at least, all those who weren't in wheelchairs or on crutches. In that moment it became obvious just how many disabled and sick people were crammed into every available space in the building. It was a sobering and yet awe-inspiring sight; each face filled with anticipation and joy. The piano started up and a deafening crescendo reverberated around the massive auditorium as thousands of voices joined to sing God's praises. Darragh was leading from a makeshift pulpit, waving his arms extravagantly to keep everyone in time with the music whilst Edsor thundered out the notes of our best-loved hymns on the grand piano.[14] I remember being fascinated by the enthusiasm of the pianist because I had already been playing the organ at our church services for a year or more by that time.'

'Then it was time for George Jeffreys to preach. You could feel the air being sucked out of the atmosphere as people held their breath in anticipation of what was to come. I was only 12 years old but I listened intently to every word the evangelist uttered. He preached the good news that Jesus came to this earth not only to die for the sins of all mankind, which in itself was marvellous and

---

[14] We tended to refer to people by their surnames in those days.

wonderful, but also to heal the broken-hearted and give sight to the blind, to restore hearing to the deaf and raise up the lame and infirm from their sickbeds. It was *"all about Jesus,"* he told us. *"He is the Saviour of the world; the Healer of our bodies; our Baptiser and one day Jesus will come again to reign on the earth."'*

'A roar of expectancy exploded across the auditorium as George Jeffreys invited all those who wanted God to heal them to make their way to the front and down the central aisle. Then he began to lay his hands on head after head as he passed down the lines, stopping here and there under the anointing of God to pray specifically over individuals.'

'There was so much going on all around, it was hard to cope with all the excitement. We had seen several impressive miracles at our own home Assembly in North Wingfield, but never anything on this scale. When he came near to where we were sitting, I could see only his back and Darragh was facing us, standing behind each person as George Jeffreys prayed, in case anyone fell backwards under the healing power of God. People were going down all over the place! It was powerful stuff.'

'I remember thinking that it must have felt just as thrilling, being in the crowds witnessing Jesus healing the sick. Emotions were running high and people were pressing in on all sides, trying to be next in line for prayer or simply wanting a better view. I was only a short lad and it was hard for me to see over the adult's heads, so I could sympathise fully with Zacchaeus[15] when he climbed the tree to see Jesus — because I was longing to stand on my chair! Yet it was impossible to be disappointed because it soon became evident that people in various parts of the auditorium were waving crutches in the air and shouting for joy. Other miracles were less obvious but just as powerful for those experiencing them.'

'During the Birmingham Campaign over 10,000 converts were registered, over 1,000 cases of miraculous healing and 1,100 candidates were immersed in water.[16] Now that's what I call a phenomenal result! You didn't go to George Jeffrey's meetings and get nothing.'

'I saw George Jeffreys three more times after that at the Elim Easter Convention meetings at Kingsway Central Hall in London. The venue was always crowded with lots happening including huge baptism services. In every meeting George would pray for the sick and it was terrific to hear him preach the Gospel with his pronounced Welsh accent. At one of these conventions I bought a record of George Jeffreys preaching, which inspired my wife Hilda and I for many years, every time we listened to it.'

Here are just a few of the people who later testified to being healed during the George Jeffreys crusade meetings in Birmingham, as recorded by Darragh. If possible, I encourage the reader to read *'In Defence of His Word'* for fuller accounts of these testimonies; the

---

[15] Luke 19:1-9.
[16] Statistics recorded in the Elim publication 'In Defense of His Word' compiled by R.E. Darragh

list provided here is to convey the *broad range* of healings experienced during the Birmingham campaign:

- ❖ Mrs A. Dodd — healed of dropsy following a bout of rheumatic fever.

- ❖ Mrs Ratcliff — healed of cancer of the throat.

- ❖ Aubrey Shellard aged 8 — healed of paralysis of the left arm, hand and leg after an accident in which he was nearly drowned.

- ❖ Mrs Rea — healed of sugar diabetes and a tumour near the heart.

- ❖ Mrs Ball — healed of septic poisoning.

- ❖ Mrs Trigg — healed of deafness, an enlarged heart and also a fibrous growth in the chest.

- ❖ Mrs Ruth Frankum — a cripple healed after thirty years of intense agony having one leg 4" shorter than the other and a badly deformed hip. She had refused to have her leg amputated. When George Jeffreys anointed Ruth with oil and prayed, her leg grew instantly and 2 days later she walked 1½ miles without the aid of a stick!

- ❖ Miss Jane Lynas — healed of heart trouble.

- ❖ Miss Agnes Radcliffe — healed of paralysis.

❖ Mrs E. Faulkner — healed of a growth in the throat.

❖ Miss K. Faulkner — defective eyesight healed after wearing glasses for 14 years.

❖ Marjory Heley — a young girl healed after suffering for 2 years with acute myeloid leukaemia; she had been diagnosed as "a hopeless case".

❖ Maureen Tinmouth — instantly healed of infantile paralysis and able to walk unaided after being in leg irons for 6 years.

❖ Joan Tinmouth — instantly healed of a tubercular spine and the fits resulting from it.

❖ Mrs E. Butler — healed of rheumatoid arthritis after suffering years of pain.

❖ Mr Edgar Hubbard — completely healed of paralysis.

❖ Miss Doris Ford — healed of nerve trouble and depression.

❖ Mrs M.J. Lucas — healed of a tumour after suffering for nine years.

❖ Mrs Johnson — cripple healed after being unable to walk without a stick for 6 years.

❖ Miss G. Whereat — healed of deafness and defective eyesight.

❖ Mrs A.E. Smith — healed after suffering for 18 years with acute neuritis.

- ❖ Mrs R.M. Mountford — healed of rheumatoid arthritis and nephritis after suffering 4½ years of agony, unable to bear anyone touching her and having been confined to bed most of the time with swollen feet and locked joints. She accepted Jesus as her Saviour, was prayed for by George Jeffreys and was healed by the power of God.

- ❖ Mrs F. Core — wonderfully healed of tumours.

- ❖ Mrs F. Hopkins — healed of a tumour.

- ❖ Mrs Hopkins' son was also remarkably healed — in May 1918 aged 11 months he had been operated on for fluid on the knee; he was put in plaster for 6 months in 1921; then he wore leg irons night and day for 8 years from 1922 to 1930. 4 days after being prayed for by George Jeffreys, he removed his leg irons and found that he could bend his knee and walk.

- ❖ Miss Emily Nicholls — healed of asthma.

- ❖ Mrs E. Nicholls — healed of rheumatism.

- ❖ Miss E. Weston — healed of defective eyesight.

- ❖ Miss E. Levick — had the use restored to a paralysed hand.[17]

- ❖ Miss Alice Sturley — healed of a dislocated hip. Alice had fallen downstairs when only 18 months old and no one realised that she had dislocated her hip. She did not begin to

[17] Matthew 12:9-14 describes Jesus healing a man with a shriveled hand.

walk until she was 3 and then only by dragging her left leg along. The doctors said they could not operate because she had a weak heart and they told her mother that Alice would not live to be 11 years of age. She did survive, but in great pain and frequently she would fall down without warning. When Alice was 16 she was given a surgical boot to assist her to walk but even so, night after night she could not sleep because of persistent pain in the right leg, which had to carry her entire weight most of the time. Over the years her dislocated left hip had become terribly swollen and much larger than the right hip, so that it gave her a twisted, unbalanced appearance. On the afternoon when she was taken to the George Jeffreys campaign meeting, Alice was the first to be prayed for. She began to tremble from head to toe. On her way home, she felt a prickly sensation and twitching in her left hip, and then in her left knee. By the time she reached her house, she found that the bone in her enlarged left hip had gone back into its socket and when her mother examined her body, both hips were the same size. After her healing Alice had to borrow the money to buy some normal shoes. She was so happy to leave off the heavy surgical boot and was very proud to stand on the church platform and hold the boot up for all to see.

❖ Miss M. Frost — healed after suffering for 6 years with defective eyesight.

- ❖ Miss Doris Cox — healed of eczema after suffering with this for 7 years.

- ❖ Miss Edna Brooks — healed of a rupture.

- ❖ Albert Spray — a young lad healed of stiff joints.

- ❖ Mrs E. Starkey — healed of rheumatoid arthritis after being very weak and unable to do her own housework. For 6 years her knees were locked and she could not kneel. She suffered acute pain and tried many remedies but nothing worked. After being prayed for, she stooped and something gave way in her knee. Afterwards she found that she could kneel again and her strength returned so that she could work.

- ❖ Mrs Shipley — healed after suffering for years with fluid in the legs. She was also healed of an ulcerated stomach.

- ❖ Mrs Simmon — completely healed of a growth diagnosed 6 years earlier. She had also worn a surgical belt for 20 years.

- ❖ Mrs Bennett — wonderfully healed of incurable heart trouble after not being able to lie down in bed for over 3 years. The doctor had told her she would never lie down again, but after being prayed for, she was able to lie flat without discomfort.

- ❖ Miss M. Welkes — healed of a growth under one knee.

- ❖ Miss R.M. Portman — healed of gastric ulcers and colitis.

❖ Mrs Potter — healed after suffering 17½ years with a tubercular hip. During that time she had spent six months in splints in a hospital bed, followed by 5 years using crutches. A fall left her in hospital for a further year, lying in a plaster case. After that she needed crutches again. At the George Jeffreys Birmingham Campaign she was anointed with oil and prayed for. God wonderfully touched her and delivered her from all pain so that she could sleep, enjoy her meals and walk without the need for splints, crutches or even a stick.

❖ Miss W. Belcher — healed of a mastoid abscess in the ear. This ear had no drum and was completely deaf. After prayer the eardrum was restored and afterwards she could hear even a watch tick.

❖ Mrs Breechshaw — healed of skin disease.

Miss Doris Coombes — healed of tubercular arthritis. At only 14 she began to suffer pain in her left arm and her school friends noticed that she was losing weight. Her arm was x-rayed and it was found that she was suffering from tubercular arthritis at the elbow joint. Her arm was then put in a plaster case. Sunray treatment in a sanatorium gave no improvement. After being prayed for in Birmingham, the pain left her arm and she began to gain weight. The doctors discharged her from further treatment.'

A little boy not mentioned in the above list as being healed during those meetings nevertheless had a wonderful, life-changing experience. His name is John Hick, who later became a professor of theology at Birmingham University and also a leading theological writer. His story was told to us briefly by Desmond Cartwright who came to our home to collect missionary archive material about Willie Burton and others from the Congo Evangelistic Mission.

DESMOND CARTWRIGHT: *'People didn't just get healed but they seemed to receive an extra dose of life!'*

'John Hicks, then aged 8, was very poorly when he was taken to the George Jeffreys Birmingham Crusade in 1930. There had been around 10,000 converts in the 9-week crusade but God had reserved something very special for this little lad.'

'I met John Hicks years later in America where he now lives and he told me, *"George Jeffreys put one hand on my head and prayed with me — and I clearly saw another hand appear on top of his hand. No one else was praying for me alongside George Jeffreys, yet there were two hands on top of my head!"'*

'I found John's account truly remarkable, that a supernatural hand appeared to cover George Jeffreys' hand as he prayed for him.'

'Over the years I have personally met many of the people, many of them women, who were healed during George Jeffrey's ministry. I was keen to find out if they were still healthy. My findings were astonishing. These women didn't just get a healing but an extra dose of life, somehow – they lived on and on into their 80's and 90's, when prior to their healings many of them were suffering life-threatening diseases!'

My father's boyhood friend, Wesley, has a very personal recollection of meeting evangelist George Jeffreys' pianist:

WESLEY BEARDSMORE: *'I was bowled over when George's pianist came to stay with us.'*

'George Jeffreys held a week's campaign at South Normanton in Derbyshire when I was a lad. It was held in the old Methodist Bethel Chapel at the invitation of Pastor George Oldershaw because our church building was not large enough to take the expected crowds. The thing I remember most about that campaign was that my hero Edsor came to stay at our house and he actually played our piano. What an honour! My best buddy, Walter Hawkins, had begged to stay with us too and we all stood around the piano singing the good old gospel songs that we knew and loved. As budding musicians, Walter and I were both keen to pick up any tips we could from Edsor's playing. Of course, no one else could get a look-in because Edsor used every key on the piano. He was the cat's whiskers!'

'Later on when I was in my late teens, George Jeffreys held a campaign in Nottingham, which ultimately led to the formation of the Elim City Temple there. They used to hold "After-Church" meetings in the cinema at Beeston in Nottingham on Sunday nights and a crowd of us used to rush over from South Normanton after our Sunday evening Gospel Service to attend them because by then my father had a car - quite a luxury in those days! My Dad hardly ever drove the car but as soon as I passed my test, naturally I took every opportunity to drive, and soon afterwards my pal Walter passed his test in our car as well.'

'The "After-Church" meetings in Beeston were fantastic and whenever George Jeffreys was there, we could hardly wait to see what would happen next, the power of God was so strongly manifested.'

'I also drove a group of friends and family to see George's brother, William Jeffreys, preaching and praying for the sick both at South Normanton and in Mansfield, Nottinghamshire where I witnessed quite a few people being healed of their ailments. What a privilege to see God's power so evidently manifested!'

'Edward Jeffreys was on the platform to help and support George but I never saw him in action. Apparently, he was preaching mainly in the Potteries around Stoke.'

'Those days when the Jeffreys brothers were touring Britain were phenomenally inspiring for Walter and me as young men; they galvanised us into action to serve God in our own generation and later we both became missionaries to the Belgian Congo.'

Stephen Jeffreys

Stephen Jeffreys was a simple Welshman born on 2nd September 1876 into a small mining community in Maesteg, Glamorganshire. He was the third child of 12 and along with many youngsters of his time he was obliged to enter the mines with his father at only 12 years of age to help support the growing family. There he toiled for 16 years - a tough apprenticeship, indeed!

But when he was 28, Stephen was powerfully converted to Christianity during the Welsh revival of 1904 and soon afterwards God gave him an overwhelming passion for lost souls accompanied by a healing ministry that can only be described as truly astonishing. He began witnessing and preaching in his home town until one day he was invited to take a 3-day mission in Cwmtwrch near Swansea, which extended into a 7-week marathon due to the crowds flocking in from all around.

"Another Welsh Revival seems to be breaking out in South Wales," reported the Confidence Magazine in January 1913. The following month the magazine described how people had walked for miles across the hills despite torrential rain to hear this young evangelist preach and many people were accepting Jesus Christ as their Saviour. Christians in small chapels all across Wales began praying that the revival would spread — and it soon did.

The first recorded healing took place when Stephen Jeffreys was preaching in Pen-y-Bont in Radnorshire, where he was asked to pray for a young woman with a cripplingly painful diseased bone in her foot that confined her to lying day after day on the sofa. Immediately when Stephen Jeffreys prayed with her, the pain left and she was able to walk unaided.

However, Stephen was always at pains to explain that the source of healing power was from Jesus alone. *'If any of you think you are coming to me to be healed, don't come near this platform,'* he would say. *'I never healed anyone in my life and never shall. Jesus is the only Healer. If you believe that, come along and I will pray for you.'*

Word soon spread about the healing that took place in Pen-y-Bont, so Stephen Jeffreys was invited to take some meetings in Llanelly. The mission was expected to last a few weeks but Stephen stayed there preaching for 7 years!

It was in Llanelly that a remarkable event took place one Sunday evening in July 1914. Stephen Jeffreys was preaching in the Island Place Mission Hall from Philippians 3:10 — *"That I might know Him, and the power of His resurrection and the fellowship of His sufferings ..."* — when suddenly on the wall behind him appeared the clear, life-like impression of a Lamb's head. People were staring at the image, which continued quite a while for all to see.

Nowadays, we would just assume that someone was projecting an image onto the wall but this was in 1914, long before DVDs, blogs, satellites and giant multi-screen displays. The image then began to change into the face of Jesus. His face was described as being *"of singular beauty, sorrowful in expression, yet enshrouded with glory"*[18]. This image remained on the wall behind the platform for several hours during which time many people examined it.

Soon people began to converge on the hall as word of the phenomenon rapidly spread and the organizers had to lock the doors for fear of a stampede. Even when everyone had left and the lights were turned out, the vision remained clearly visible. Disappointed, the rapidly growing crowd became more and more insistent, until finally everyone was allowed inside in an orderly fashion. The vision of Jesus as "The Man of Sorrows" was still there. Many fell to their knees in contrition, overwhelmed by a sense of their own sinfulness.

Stephen Jeffreys wanted to know the meaning of such an astonishing vision. He knew that it must have enormous significance, so he began to pray and ask God to reveal the meaning of it to him, much as Daniel did when the vision of a hand writing the words *"Mene, Mene, Tekel, Parsin"* appeared on the palace wall in Babylon during King Belshazzar's banquet.[19] God showed Stephen that the vision was a portent of great suffering. A month later, the First World War commenced.

Stephen had such a mighty faith in God's power after this that he feared nothing. He was willing to lay hands on all types of sickness, much as Jesus did in the Bible, without prejudice or fear.

---

[18]From "The Sound of a Going" by Alfred Missen. Assemblies of God Publishing House, 1973.
[19] Daniel 5:1-30

Whether it was blindness, paralysis, deafness, cancers — all these things fled as he prayed for people to be healed.

My father's childhood friend, Wesley Beardsmore, recalls a memorable healing that took place in Mansfield of a man dying with stomach cancer. This man had suffered with serious internal disease for some time and had all but given up hope. His doctors had nothing more to offer him other than palliative care. Then he heard of the Stephen Jeffrey's meetings and clutched at this last straw. Standing in the line to be prayed for, he hardly dared to believe that this Jesus whom Stephen Jeffreys was preaching about really loved him or would stoop down to touch him; his self-esteem was so low, his hopes and dreams shattered by terminal illness. As if Stephen Jeffreys could feel this man's pain and doubt, he asked him if he truly believed that Jesus could heal his disease.

'I think so — I hope so,' the man stammered self-consciously. His sunken eyes told a different story.

From where Wesley sat, the prospect seemed bleak.

Stephen Jeffreys immediately called for the congregation to start singing a faith-inspiring hymn. As the people worshipped, a wave of faith and expectancy began to sweep through the room. Then Stephen laid his hands on the man's bloated stomach and commanded the cancer to shrink.

That was it; there were many others to be prayed for and Stephen moved on down the line. Young Wesley was disappointed because it was impossible for him to see any changes taking place in the man because the sickness was internal.

Perhaps this is why, night after night, people would return to hear the testimonies of people who had been healed and to hear Stephen Jeffreys preach.

In Mansfield, the man with stomach cancer later returned to praise God for his healing. The doctors had been mystified when his jaundiced skin rapidly returned to a normal healthy colour. He began eating normally and continued to live. Later tests proved that the cancer had shrunk to a fraction of its former size. In time all traces of the cancer disappeared. The man was totally healed.

Not everyone was healed who stood in the prayer lines but hundreds did receive miraculous healings during his short period of ministry. Through it all, he remained a humble servant of God.

DONALD GEE: *'It all happened where he was concerned in a space of less than 7 years.'*

'Stephen Jeffreys was inimitable; Christ's gift of an evangelist. That blending of humour and pathos, of unpolished eloquence with passionate evangelism made him mighty in God.'

'I first met Stephen Jeffreys personally when I was invited by Cecil Polhill to play the piano for the healing campaign being held in Horbury Chapel (now Kensington Temple) in West London. I remember watching the row of fascinated Congregationalist deacons standing on the back pews to get a better view of what was happening in the front as the evangelist laid hands on the sick. An almighty cheer went up when we saw the incredulous smile broadening on the face a deaf man as he realized that for the first time he could hear what the man of God was saying! It was a delightful and memorable healing.'

'Later in 1926, Stephen Jeffreys came to stay at my house during his campaign in Edinburgh. His vitality amazed me. After each strenuous meeting preaching and praying for the sick, he would come home with me and be full of life and fun. But during the days he would ask me to drive him out to the Firth of Forth for several hours of solitude and complete quietness where he could recuperate physically and spiritually. His preaching was so powerful that at the closing meeting I saw men literally grasping the seat in front of them in terror as the evangelist preached on the judgment to come.'

'In many ways Stephen Jeffreys was reminiscent of one of the old Hebrew prophets that we read of in the Bible. Despite his irrepressible wit and humour he could also on occasion be most forthright and terrible. I recall traveling to hear him at a Whitsuntide Convention meeting in the Kingsway Hall, London where he proclaimed doom on this unrepentant city. Fourteen years later his words burned in my memory as I walked through the charred and ruined streets of the City of London after the great air raids of 1941.'

'In 1928 he started off on a World Tour of ministry on land and by sea. I preceded him to New Zealand where I was asked to help prepare for his forthcoming crusades by telling the churches about the many healings and miracles witnessed in his great British campaigns. He and I spoke briefly on the telephone before I sailed from Auckland. God was using him mightily in countries around the world even in those early years before air travel made it possible for the emergence of 'world evangelists' such as Billy Graham.'

'Stephen Jeffreys had a few more good healing campaigns after he returned to England but the dynamism of the old days never fully returned. Sadly, his health began to fail early and by the time he was 59 he was crippled with arthritis. His closing years were spent back in his native South Wales, where I visited him in his small home in Porthcawl. I was glad to see that he was being lovingly cared for by his wife and daughter.'

'As we prayed together, it was a most moving experience for me to place my hands on his gnarled, shriveled fingers and to recall how those very same hands had been placed with tremendous healing power upon thousands whom God had healed during his ministry. These are mysteries before which we are wiser to be silent.'

'For the present generation Stephen Jeffreys cannot be more than a name, and almost a legend, but to their grandfathers he was always the "Beloved Evangelist".'[20]

WALTER: *'It was one of the most remarkable healings I have ever witnessed.'*

---

[20] From his personal memoirs "These Men I Knew", Assemblies of God Publishing House, 1980.

'Stephen Jeffreys held a campaign in our home town of Chesterfield in the summer of 1928 when I was only a strip of a lad, just 10 years old. Oh, those were meetings I will never forget! We sang rousing choruses such as …'

Everybody ought to love Jesus, Jesus, Jesus
He died on the tree to set us free
Everybody ought to love Jesus
and

Rolled away, rolled away
And the burden of my heart rolled away
Every sin had to go beneath the cleansing flow
Hallelujah! Rolled away, rolled away
And the burden of my heart rolled away

'… which always remind me of those special times. We were on the edge of our seats with expectancy. You could feel the presence of God with Stephen Jeffreys as he walked into the hall; he had such power, such charisma. Most people had arrived very early to make sure of getting a seat and the place was packed out.'

'As he began to speak, Stephen Jeffreys told us that during the week before the Chesterfield Crusade was due to start, he had received a life-changing revelation when he climbed the Welsh mountain near his home to spend time alone in prayer. After admiring the stunning views across the valleys and hills beyond, he had lain down on a grassy slope looking up at the clouds swirling overhead. He was so moved by the beauty and grandeur all around him that he cried out, *"Oh God, I am such a worm compared with what You have done in Creation!"*'

'The power of God fell on Stephen and in that moment he realised, not just in his head but deep down in his soul, *"If God can create all that, **nothing is impossible to Him**."'*

'He had come straight from this profound revelation on the mountain to the Chesterfield meetings and that evening he dispensed with the normal routine of preaching the Gospel before praying for the sick. Instead, he explained what had happened to him on the mountain and then he simply said, *"There are many of you here who are burdened with sickness and disease. God wants to heal you. Come down to the front right now and I will pray for you."'*

'I wanted to stand on my seat; I was so excited and anxious to see what was going to happen and my parents had to hold me down! We were all craning our necks for the best view possible as the great evangelist left the platform to meet the surging crowd flocking to the front. Little did Stephen Jeffreys know that the very first challenge he would have to face there in Chesterfield Market Hall was a mother leading her sightless son to the front to be prayed for.'

'The lad was about my age and he had absolutely no eyes in his empty sockets. As the mother explained that her son was born without eyes, you could see that Stephen Jeffreys had such tender love for the boy. His own eyes brimming with tears, Stephen put his thumb into one empty socket and his first finger in the other, and then he looked up and prayed to his Father in Heaven to whom nothing is impossible.'

'Instantly the miracle happened. As Stephen Jeffreys removed his hand from the boy's face, the lad had 2 beautiful blue eyes and I saw it first hand and close up! His mother couldn't stop weeping for joy — her son could now see perfectly. The crowd, from being silent in eager suspense, burst into a tumultuous roar of praise and worship. Praise God — it was awesome being with my parents and most of the members of our church witnessing such a tremendous miracle. We were cheering and clapping, and jumping up and down. Many of us were standing on our chairs by then for a better view — we didn't want to miss a thing!'

'The boy stared in wonderment — first at Stephen Jeffreys who had just prayed for him, then at the bright lights, the cheering crowd, and finally he turned to his mother with rapture in his face as he saw her for the very first time. I remember that he reached up his arms and gave her the biggest hug. The place erupted again, everyone cheering and hollering and praising God. Mother and son wept together, squeezing each other with delight.'

'She must have said something like, "*Let me have a look at you, son*" because they separated and as she gazed lovingly into her son's blue eyes, tears flooded out of her own and she began sobbing with pure gratitude, "*Jesus, Jesus, Jesus! Oh, thank you Jesus! Oh, praise God!*" The pair were hugging and jumping up and down with joyful abandon, praising the Lord with the rest of us. It was a creative miracle of the highest order.'

'By then more and more people were filling the aisle behind the pair wanting Stephen Jeffreys to pray for them also. They were almost crushing the lad in their enthusiasm to reach the front, so his mother steered him through the crowd back to their seat, and I could see clearly the tears streaming down both their faces as they passed by our row.'

This was by no means the only miracle seen during the Chesterfield Campaign. Since my grandparents and father lived nearby, they were at most of the meetings. Here is my father's account of another amazing miracle that took place during that crusade:

WALTER: *'Stephen Jeffreys was not afraid to pray for anyone. He just trusted God to heal.'*

'At another of the meetings in Chesterfield Market Hall, I can remember that as the meeting was about to start, a paralysed man from Somercotes was carried in on a stretcher, brought to the front and lifted up onto the platform. I was utterly amazed to think that the man's relatives had enough faith to bring such a sick person and struggle as they did to manhandle the heavy stretcher up onto the massive stage. It reminded me of the account in the Bible[21] when some men lifted a cripple onto the roof of the house where Jesus was teaching because they could not get near to Him for the massive

[21] Mark 2:1-12

crowd standing all around. They dug a hole in the roof and, using the mat that he was laid on, lowered the paralysed man down in front of Jesus. I guess that the crowd in that room felt a bit like I did — it seemed a bit of a cheek somehow, but very brave of them at the same time. I was so excited; I couldn't wait to see what was going to happen!'

'It didn't seem to faze Stephen Jeffreys one bit when he walked into the hall to find his platform cluttered with this very sick man stretched out in front of him.'

'Before praying for the sick, Stephen Jeffreys began to preach from the Bible about the Widow of Nain's Son[22] whom Jesus raised from the dead. He related the account of how Jesus happened to meet a funeral procession coming out of a town called Nain and had compassion on the widow who was weeping because she was about to bury her only son.'

'Stephen Jeffreys stopped in the middle of his sermon, then he said these words very pointedly, "*Jesus spoke to the corpse on the stretcher and said to him, «Young man, I say unto thee arise» — and he did! And Jesus restored him to his mother.*"'

'Then Stephen Jeffreys turned to Mr. Wright, this inert figure on the stretcher. He took Mr. Wright by the hand and looking into his eyes, loudly pronounced the words of our Lord, "*Young man, I say unto **thee** arise!*"'

---

[22] Luke 7:11-17

'Mr. Wright, who had been totally unable to move until that moment, gradually leaned forward. With Stephen Jeffreys still holding his hand, he slipped one leg over the side of his stretcher followed by the other leg and then he slowly stood up.'

'The crowd roared in praise to God. Stephen Jeffreys walked with Mr. Wright to the end of the platform and back again, still holding his hand. Then he let go and went back to the pulpit to continue preaching. Meantime, Mr. Wright continued to walk up and down the platform behind Stephen Jeffreys.'

'It was really hard for me as a 10-year-old lad to concentrate on the message after that, because my eyes were following Mr. Wright's progress. I think everyone else was the same. It was amazing! Here was a man, formerly paralysed and unable to walk, wandering back and forth across the platform, obviously getting stronger with every step, dressed only in his nightshirt!'

'Our church was buzzing for months, even years, after that Crusade. The whole experience had a profound influence on my young life and paved the way for me in my own ministry to have enough faith to dare to lay hands on the sick in the Name of Jesus and see them recover.'

HILDA: *'My best friend knew Mr. Wright very well. He lived in her village.'*

'We were all very excited at our little church at Bonsall about the Stephen Jeffrey's Campaign in Chesterfield. I was only 9 years old at the time but I wanted to hear every detail about the great preacher who had come to our area and I was especially interested to hear accounts of all the healings that took place. Some people from our church went to see him preach.'

'My best friend, Rita Kay, told me all about Mr. Wright being healed. He had been totally paralysed and nurses were caring for him all the time. Everyone knew about his deteriorating condition in the village of Somercotes where Rita lived.'

'I can't remember now whether she said that he had come straight from the hospital, or whether they had taken him home first. All I know is that he was lying on a stretcher and his family brought him all the way to Chesterfield Market Hall in the back of a butcher's van! Then they carried him straight up onto the platform without any bye or leave.'

'When Stephen Jeffrey's prayed for Mr. Wright to be healed right in the middle of his sermon, the poor man was a bit embarrassed because he had only his bedclothes on and when he tried to get up off the stretcher his blankets got in the way! Can you imagine walking up and down in front of hundreds of people dressed only in a nightshirt? It's everyone's nightmare! But I don't suppose he was too concerned about that once he realised that he could sit up and walk after being paralysed and bedridden for so long.'

'Rita said that the whole of Somercotes knew that a miracle had taken place because Mr. Wright was walking around for all to see. They were talking about it for weeks on every street corner, in the churches, in shops, pubs and wherever people met. Even strangers would start talking about the miracle when they were queuing at the Post Office for their pensions or sitting next to each other on the bus.'

'Those were great days for us Pentecostals. For me it was so exciting to realise for the first time as a young child that God loves us all so much that He sent Jesus to die for us, not only to forgive us of our sins but also to heal our diseases. It made me thrilled to be a Christian.

CHAPTER 2:

A Miraculous Conception

'If you obey God and you believe God, it's amazing what God will do.' Ps.
GERARD KEEHAN[23]

Nowadays, the term 'miracle baby' is quite common, usually reserved for babies who survive against incredible odds to become normal infants. With the amazing scientific advances of past decades and improved medical care, the boundaries of what may be considered to be an extraordinary conception or birth are constantly being pushed back, so that what may have seemed almost impossible to achieve only a few years ago is now quite commonplace.

There are now multitudes of so-called 'test tube babies' and had I been born today, I could well have been one of them. However, in 1950, the scenario for my parents was bleak, with adoption being the only plausible solution for a childless couple in their predicament.

From my earliest recollections, I have always known that I was special. Being an only child, I was always the *'apple of my father's eye'* and my mother's *'precious gift from God'*, but their love went far beyond that of parents who have borne their children with

---

[23] With his wife, Sue, founder of Globalheart Church – *'A local church in three global locations'* (Australia, Zambia & Germany)

relative ease, for to them I was a true 'miracle baby' in every sense of the word.

Our story spans two continents. It involves years of private prayer watered by a substantial sprinkling of faith. The Bible teaches us that prayer is a powerful tool that brings results.[24] Let my mother tell you what happened in her own words.

HILDA: *'Becoming a mother was a real test of my faith.'*

'My husband and I were childhood sweethearts. I can remember the day I first set eyes on Walter Hawkins. He was eleven years old and I was just ten, a year and a day his junior. I was playing a game of 'rounders' on the village street with my friends when I observed a young boy in a smart navy suit turn the corner and pop a letter into the post box that was inset into the boundary wall of Chestnuts Farm where I lived. In a small village like Bonsall in Derbyshire, news travels fast and I soon learned that the lad had come to stay with Miss Byard, a good friend and neighbour of ours. She was his great aunt.'

'The very next Sunday, my parents were holding a special Communion Service at our farm and there was to be an important visiting preacher. Our front parlour was crammed full of guests, so I was not allowed in. Out of curiosity, I sat on the stairs watching a procession of newcomers arriving and being greeted at the door with

---

[24] James 5:16 'The earnest prayer of a righteous person has great power and produces wonderful results.' NLT

great warmth and kisses. Then I spotted the dapper little boy in the navy suit entering with his Bible tucked under one arm. He looked much smaller and younger than me, so immediately I ran into the kitchen to complain to my mother, who had assured me that this gathering was not for children. Eventually, after much pleading, I persuaded her to allow me to take a kitchen stool into the room if I could find a space. *But where to sit?* I surveyed the crowded parlour with its large bay window full to capacity and saw that the little boy was perched next to his parents at the end of the front row by the fireplace, so with no more ado I plonked my stool right beside him. I said nothing and just sat there, pleased as can be.'

'I have never had eyes for any other man since that first meeting. It seemed that Walter's parents became attracted to Bonsall village almost as much as Walter and I became attracted to each other. I was a shy farm lass and he a miner's son with a difference; his father was also a vocational minister and Walter's talents soon made room for him. By the age of twelve, Walter was already teaching a Bible Class of lads up to fourteen years old and he was also the church organist in North Wingfield Assembly, Derbyshire. We were to see each other several times a year after our first meeting and by the age of fourteen, I was writing Walter love poems and we were exchanging greeting cards.'

'During the ensuing war years, I trained in Leeds as a midwife earning five shillings a week, and later became a staff nurse at Willersley Castle. Meantime Walter became an accredited minister, completing his training at a church in Belper, Derbyshire and then working as a pastor in Willington, County Durham in the north east of England. There were many lonely months of separation but we kept in touch by letter.'

'I recollect that one time he wrote to me saying, "*Oh, by the way, I must tell you that I married a lovely young lady on Saturday!*"'

'I was ready with my reply. "*Well, what do you think? I had a baby last Saturday!*" Little did I realise how those words, written in jest, would return to haunt me in the years that followed. It all seemed so easy then; after all, women were giving birth in our busy maternity hospital on a daily basis.'

'Walter proposed marriage to me in the little church within the Willersley Castle grounds. We prayed earnestly together and made our plans to serve the Lord as missionaries to the Congo.'

'It seemed a happy coincidence that Walter and myself had met for the first time in our lovely big front room at Chestnuts Farm, for fifteen long years later we became the joyful bride and groom presiding at our own wedding reception in that same room with seventy guests packed tightly in. My mother had prepared a veritable feast for us despite the wartime rationing.'

'Walter and I spent the first four years of our marriage in the centre of Africa, concentrating on learning the Kiluba language and putting our whole lives into our missionary work. It had been a perilous voyage in a convoy of twenty-three merchant ships, zigzagging across the north Atlantic and down the west coast of Africa in an attempt to dodge the German U-boats. After only sixteen weeks on our Mission Station at Kabondo-Dianda, Walter was able to preach his first faltering sermon in Kiluba and subsequently he set about visiting villages throughout the region, teaching and preaching the Gospel. Meantime I pioneered a midwifery work among the local women.'

'Life was tough. At first, we had only a simple hovel in which to live; it did not even have a door to protect us from wild beasts as we slept, and a massive anthill rose from the centre of the bedroom floor right up to the mud ceiling! The entire roof was heaving with ants and in the two habitable rooms, the dirt floors dipped in the middle where the earth had been swept away. Our hearts sank as we settled in. We had to use our packing crates for furniture and Walter rigged up a bamboo lattice mat to cover the open doorway. The place was a haven for mosquitoes, cockroaches, mice and rats. On our first night there, I placed my new shoes by our bedside and in the morning found that they had been attacked by termites during the night. Termites had also eaten the spine of Walter's Bible, which was practically falling apart. It was hardly a promising beginning!'

'Needless to say, Walter soon improved our humble abode by constructing a new thatched roof with the help of local villagers, and adding cement floors, wooden doors and mosquito net windows. He even built a separate cookhouse nearby with a corrugated iron roof so that I could cook indoors safely and later he erected a simple building to accommodate my midwifery clinic.'

'Our lives were full, yet it was a great sadness to us during that first term in the Congo that our desire to start a family had not been realised. Day after day, my arms had been filled with beautiful Congolese babies and I had cried tears of joy with the families at each successful birth, yet deep inside, I was yearning for a child of our own.'

'"*What could be wrong?*" Walter and I discussed this many times and eventually decided that perhaps when we returned to the more temperate climate in England for our first yearlong furlough, it would give us a chance to recuperate and things would right themselves naturally. Perhaps then we would be able to conceive.'

'We returned to England in August 1948 full of hope. Much of our time was spent itinerating around the country raising funds for the mission in Congo. In our spare time we visited relatives and relaxed as much as possible, but as the weeks passed by there were still no signs of a pregnancy. By that time we had been married for almost five years and Walter and I began to pray even more earnestly than ever before. I could not bear to return to Africa childless with my arms empty, where I would be facing the prospect of delivering at least ten babies a week for the women in my care.'

'In November 1948 we came to a joint decision: we would wait for another six months to allow God to intervene in our situation and then if there was still no sign of a pregnancy, we would try to adopt a baby before returning to Congo. Reverently, we agreed together in prayer and made our solemn promise before God to wait a further six months for His help before making any effort to adopt. Our deadline was set for the end of May 1949.'

'Soon after we made our pledge, Walter's mother informed us that she had heard of someone who was looking for a good home for a baby that would be born and given up for adoption in February. Walter and I looked at each other in astonishment. No one, not even his mother, knew at that stage that we were contemplating adopting a baby. We took a little time to pray and steady our resolve. It was not an easy decision, but because of the pact we had made with each other and before God, reluctantly Walter and I declined the opportunity for ourselves and suggested another childless missionary couple who were our close friends. They were only too delighted to adopt the baby girl after she was born. Her name was Molly. I visited their home later that spring, and when I held little Molly in my arms, my heart cried out to God in desperation. She was so beautiful.'

'At around the same time, we heard that my brother Oswald and his wife Joan had taken fertility tests at their local hospital. They had been married six months longer than us and were obviously in the same predicament as ourselves. When the test results came through, Oswald and Joan were delighted to learn that there was no reason at all why they should not be able to conceive children. The whole family rejoiced.'

'It took a little courage on our part, but inspired by this happy turn of events, Walter and I decided that we, too, should seek medical advice to determine why we had not been able to conceive a baby. We hoped as always for good news. Our doctor referred us to Derby General Hospital for fertility testing and a week later we returned for our results. The consultant looked sombre. He cleared his throat and regretfully informed us that not just one, but both, of us had problems. What a shock! It took a while for the dreadful news to sink in… we were both infertile.'

'Huge disappointment set in after that. We had just lost a significant opportunity to adopt a lovely baby and now, humanly speaking, it appeared impossible for us to conceive our own child. May 1949 came and went, and the deadline passed. The second part of our plan had been to adopt but now it seemed that there was no child available. Time was running out for us as we were due to return to Africa before the end of the year, but somehow we kept clinging to the faint hope that God might yet perform a miracle for us one way or another, so we continued to wait.'

'At the end of August, I had a visit from a dear friend who was expecting her first baby in the autumn. During her stay, I asked her to pray with me that I, too, would become pregnant despite the consultant's hopeless prognosis. She was just going out to the shops to buy four baby vests, first size. I reached for my purse and asked her in faith to buy me four additional vests for the baby that Walter and I were trusting in God to conceive.'

'"*Are you sure?*" she asked.'

'"*Yes,*" I said. "*Please do this for me.*"'

'Walter and I continued to pray, day after day, but still there was no sign of a baby. All autumn long we prayed. We were so sad and discouraged, yet clinging to God and hoping beyond hope for a miracle. I treasured my four little vests and wept inwardly for the child I didn't have. Little did I realise that by purchasing those baby vests, I had taken a crucial step of faith in my life. By that simple act, I was signifying to God, "*Lord, I believe that you can do this. You can make a way where there seems no way for both of us to be healed of our infertility.*"'

'In the background, Walter's mother was praying also. She was a very godly woman and although we had not shared our concerns with her, she obviously sensed that something might be wrong. Eventually she could contain her curiosity no longer.'

'"*Don't you want a baby?*" she asked me one day.'

'"*Yes, of course we do,*" I replied.'

'"*Well then, I know how to pray, now, don't I?*" she commented wryly.'

'Finally, in October 1949, Walter and I conceived our very own baby. What ecstatic joy! **Two infertilities plus God equalling one pregnancy!** What a miracle! By the end of November, we knew for sure and were thrilled to tell everybody about God's goodness to us both. It is an answer to prayer that I will remember for the rest of my days.'

Walter: *'We waited six years and then God gave us the miracle answer to our prayers.'*

'We had been due to return to Africa by the winter of 1949, but given the unusual circumstances, Hilda and I felt it was prudent to wait until our precious baby had been delivered safely before resuming our work in the Congo.'

'During the spring of 1950, I travelled to Belgium and studied to gain a better grasp of the French language, which would prove an important asset when dealing with the authorities back in the Belgian Congo. Under doctor's advice, Hilda remained at home with her parents during her pregnancy in order to take every reasonable precaution with her health. We could not afford to lose our precious miracle baby after waiting all those years.'

'Upon my return to England, I continued my itinerary around the country, preaching and gaining support for our mission in Africa. It was an anxious time. Eventually my wife went into labour and I rushed her to the hospital.'

'The next evening, I drove into the car park at the back of our little assembly hall in North Wingfield. My father was in the vestry making preparations to lead the service when I entered. He threw his arms around me excitedly:'

'"*What is it, son?*" he asked in his broad Derbyshire accent. "*A lass or a lad?*"'

'"*Neither,*" I replied. "*It's a woman!*"'

'"*What do you mean?*" he retorted, looking at me perplexed.'

'"*It was a false alarm, Dad. She hasn't had the baby yet, after all that,*" I sighed, "*So I've brought her back home.*"'

'Hilda followed me in, and she could see the look of disbelief on my father's face. We eventually all fell about laughing, but when you have been praying so hard and for so long, last minute hiccups don't go down very well in anybody's book.'

'Finally, two weeks later on July 20th 1950 at five past midday, our lovely daughter was born. She was perfect in every way. Full of gratitude for our own special miracle baby, we gave her the names Pearl (meaning 'precious') and Dorothy (meaning 'gift of God'). Truly she was, and still is, our very own precious gift from God.'

'Six weeks after Pearl was born, we began the long journey with our own little precious bundle, back to the mission field in Congo. By God's grace, there God protected her from two bouts of malaria, venomous snakes and leopard attacks, tropical storms, bush fires, and all manner of infestations and insects; such as hook worms, jiggers and bird-eating spiders. One dreadful night we found Pearl whimpering in her bed, covered in thousands of marching ants that could have eaten her alive! Through all this, God graciously protected her and us, for which we give Him thanks.'

Hilda and Walter Hawkins with miracle-baby Pearl

Years later, I met the little baby girl whom my parents declined to adopt. She, too, had been brought up in a Christian family and there seemed an uncanny affinity, somehow, between us. It was like looking at a mirage; this beautiful young woman who might have been my mother's only child instead of me, if she had been adopted at that time by my parents. It was a strange feeling and I was truly glad that my mother hadn't lost her nerve and given in to the chance to adopt when the opportunity presented itself to her. With hindsight, it is possible to see that the offer of that little baby girl for adoption was a test of my parent's faith in God and commitment to the pact they had made with each other in His presence. I feel that God rewarded their faith because they kept to their word and did not waver under pressure.

The circumstances of my conception and birth may seem fairly low key if compared to some of the examples we read of in the Bible, such as the account of Sarah[25] who gave birth to her only son Isaac when she was well past child-bearing age and her husband Abraham was a hundred years old. That takes some beating! My mother was only 31 years of age when I was born, a mere spring chicken in comparison.

However, there are similar examples to my parent's experience that are considered to be miracles in the Bible. If we examine the story of Hannah,[26] she also waited year after year for a child without success, just as my mother did. Eventually, with great bitterness of soul, Hannah went to the temple of God in Shiloh and wept before the Lord. She, like my parents, made a solemn vow before God and He heard her prayer and granted her request. Within a few months Hannah conceived a son and called him Samuel, "*Because*," she said, "*I asked the Lord for him.*" Hannah then fulfilled her vow to God by dedicating her cherished son to God's service, and Samuel eventually became a prophet and the High Priest of Israel.

It is such a privilege to know from personal experience that the God of the Bible still answers prayer today. In fact, I am living proof that Almighty God grants miracles and favours to those who

---

[25] Genesis 18:1-15 and Genesis 21:1-7
[26] 1 Samuel 1:1-19

trust Him now, in our generation, every bit as much as He did in Hannah's and Samuel's day. God responded to my parent's persistent prayers all those years ago and honoured their real faith in Him. I'm so very glad He did!

CHAPTER 3: An Audible Voice

'And He walks with me, and He talks with me /

And He tells me I am His own.' [27]

The Voice in the Field

My maternal grandfather, William Potter, was born in 1874. He was a farmer all his life and a perfect gentleman. I never once heard him raise his voice in anger or speak a harsh word. At one time, he served as a Justice of the Peace in Matlock, Derbyshire. He was also a founding member of the famous Bakewell Show, where local farmers can display or sell their produce and livestock. On top of all this, Granddad Potter was the pastor of a little AoG church in Bonsall for twenty years, which he started in the large parlour of Chestnuts Farm on Bonsall Hill, cramming about 30 members in. That is where my mother and father met, aged only 10 and 11 years old, when my Grandma Hawkins came to preach at the budding 'church on the farm'. Eventually he found premises in the village and the church is still going strong today.

---

[27] Quoted from the hymn, 'In the Garden' (C. Austin Miles, 1912) – famously recorded by Elvis Presley in 1967.

William Potter at the Bakewell Show

Granddad Potter lived to the ripe old age of 93 and God granted him his request that he should die peacefully in his sleep. His is a remarkable story:

WILLIAM: *'How I came to be saved.'*

'I was born and brought up on Harthill Farm near Bakewell in Derbyshire. My forebears had been farmers from as far back as our ancestral records began. I was the weakling of our family and my parents often despaired of ever rearing me. At birth, I was so tiny that I could fit into a 3-pint milk jug. Then at seven years of age I nearly died of scarlet fever. The doctor visited me daily and one evening he told my mother to expect the worst; he was certain that I would not live through the night. At that time, we had a maid called Lizzie Baker who was helping my mother to care for me. She was a keen Salvation Army lassie and she must have been praying for me because, contrary to all expectations, God spared my life.'

'I believe that even then, God was watching over me, because I did survive. I was so weak that I had to be pushed around in a kiddie's pushchair for quite a while afterwards and then I had to learn to walk all over again. In the ensuing years I was stricken with a succession of severe illnesses including rheumatic fever, pernicious anaemia and pneumonia, but through each of them, my life was spared.'

'In 1897, our family doctor asked permission to perform an emergency operation on our long, well-scrubbed kitchen table. In those days before reliable anaesthetics were available, only the direst cases were treated surgically. My father assisted at the operating table but when the patient's stomach was opened up, the man was so full of cancer that the doctor sewed him up again quickly. As a strange sequel to this event, both the doctor and my father contracted cancer shortly afterwards and died. I was only 22 years old and my father's untimely death at only 56 years of age troubled me greatly. I began to realise that although we attended church regularly and even had our own family pew, I had never really experienced any true relationship with God for myself. In those days, our religion was put on and taken off with our Sunday clothes.'

'My seven siblings and I took over my father's role at Harthill Farm until my mother passed away nine years later in 1906. I was the second of three sons and it was hard work with so many mouths to feed, but we managed well enough.'

'Not long before my mother died, I met with a bad accident. I had just turned 30 years of age at the time and was taking a sow to Bakewell market in our horse and trap. The sow was tied down under a heavy net at the back of the cart. She was in a vicious mood and was becoming more and more entangled in the netting. Suddenly one of the ropes securing the net gave way, and the sow shot forward and butted me from behind with her snout. I was pitched out of the cart by the force of the pig and landed head first on a rock in the road. I have no idea how long I lay there unconscious because it was a very isolated spot and no one witnessed the incident.'

'Eventually I regained consciousness and managed to sit up shakily. I remember wondering where my horse and cart were. Everything was a blur. After a while I scrambled to my feet and saw my horse standing still in the road about 50 yards away, grazing on some grass by the wayside. Somehow I was able to complete my journey despite my injuries.'

'Pondering later about what had happened, I realised that this was the fifth time that God had spared my life. It occurred to me that I could have lain in the road for hours before anyone passed that way. I could have even broken my neck or bled to death with no one to help me. I remember asking myself, *"Suppose I had been killed, what would have happened to my spirit? I might have gone to Hell!"* The shock of that realisation made me think of giving my life to God more and more as the days passed by.'

'In 1907 Harthill Farm was sold, and I moved with two of my younger sisters and one brother to Bank Farm in Upper Town, Bonsall. One by one the others left to get married and at my youngest sister Clara's wedding I met the bridegroom's older sister Florence Young. I learned of her love and devotion to her mother after her own father's death, and how capable she had been to take over the family drapery business and make a good success of it. She was 24 years old and had strikingly healthy good looks. I immediately fell in love with her.'

'Since Florrie and her mother were members of the local Baptist Chapel, and because I had such an ache in my heart to find God, I started to attend the services with them.'

'Then I had a dramatic encounter that transformed my life. One day, while walking through a field at Bank Farm, I heard a strong, clear voice at my side saying these words: "*I am Jesus speaking. I am real.*" That was all I heard. I spun round but no one was there. I was in the middle of an empty field and all about me was complete stillness. There was not a person in sight. I was so thrilled that my steps became quite light as if I were walking on a cushion of air. It was such a profound experience that I said to myself, "*If Jesus speaks again, I will give Him my heart.*"'

'For the next few days I kept thinking on these lines when Jesus spoke to me again, but not in the same way. This time He spoke directly into my heart, saying, "*Son, give me your heart.*" It was just as clear as if Jesus had spoken the words audibly like before. Immediately I cried out with a loud voice, "*I will, Lord!*" I fell to my knees and started to pray, which I had not done for many years. Tears were running down my cheeks. I rose up a changed man, redeemed. I had made my peace with God.'

'Shortly after this, Florrie and I travelled with fourteen other members of Bonsall Baptist Church to be baptised by full immersion in the baptistery at Belper. I became a member and soon was made a Deacon and Treasurer of the Bonsall Baptist Church, where I served happily for almost twenty years.' 'During that period, I married Florrie and we had two sons, Billie and Oswald, and a daughter called Hilda.

'We moved to Chestnuts Farm at the top of the hill in Bonsall. There I wrote in giant letters on our huge barn doors, "JESUS SAVES AND SATISFIES."'

'I often told people about my encounter with Jesus and the profound difference He had made in my life.'

William and Florence Potter on their wedding day

'One day in 1927 I read in the local paper about a man called Stephen Jeffreys who was holding evangelistic meetings in Chesterfield. Many people were getting healed in their bodies and accepting Jesus Christ as their Saviour. Eight of us from our Church went to see for ourselves. We returned from the meeting full of excitement for we had never seen the likes of it before! That experience made a great change in us, because we were seeing miracles just like those we read about in the Bible.'

'The result was that we started our own Breaking of Bread Services in our front room at Chestnuts Farm. On Whit Monday in May 1931, we erected a tent on our lawn for three convention meetings. We also convened two meetings in our large bedroom upstairs for seeking the Baptism of the Holy Spirit, just as they did in the upper room in the Bible.[28] Twenty-seven people received the Holy Spirit that day including Florrie and me, and we all started praising God in languages we had never learned.'

'Our daughter Hilda was one of the first among us to receive this empowering gift from God and with tears running down her cheeks, I remember my formerly shy little girl boldly praying for her mother to receive the Holy Spirit, saying, "*Mam, all you have to do is open your mouth and let Him in!*"'

'After five years of holding meetings in our homes, our little group purchased an old Primitive Methodist Chapel in Bonsall and made it our Church Hall. I was invited to become the Pastor of Bonsall Assembly, where I served for a further twenty years until I retired.'

---

[28] Acts 2:1-4.

An encounter such as this is not as rare as you may think. I have heard many people relate similar experiences where they have met Jesus, spoken with Jesus, or simply heard His audible voice as my grandfather did. From the earliest Bible times, there have been documented encounters with not only angels, who are God's messengers, but with the visible presence of God. In every recorded encounter of this nature, the person being visited is never the same again. Their life is completely transformed.

The account of when the Apostle Paul met with Jesus on the road to Damascus may have been far more dramatic than my grandfather's experience, but there are still some important similarities.[29] Each heard the audible voice of the Lord telling him, "*I am Jesus.*" Each of them was given a specific instruction; both were baptised shortly after their encounter with Jesus and both of them became ministers of the gospel.

Hilda's Comforter

My mother, Hilda Hawkins, suffered severe osteoporosis for her last ten years or so until towards the end, bent double by its cruel grip on her body, everything hurt — her knees, hips, fingers; she struggled even to breathe. Often, she would beg the Lord to take her home - saying that she couldn't imagine how to face another day in such pain. The morphine patches scarcely worked anymore and I

---

[29] Acts 9:1-19.

used to think that if she took many more pills you'd hear her rattling from down the street!

Yet God saw fit to preserve her life for a purpose. Every morning and evening, my parents faithfully prayed for us, our family, our friends and church members, along with a huge list of missionaries and Christian workers from around the world. Theirs was a valuable ministry that so few of us undertake given the demanding pace of our lives. Who would pray for this world if it were not for the likes of these precious silver-haired veterans amongst us?

Thus, the Lord spared Mum's life to be a continuing blessing and companion to my Dad until she reached nearly 93 years of age.

From time to time, God would encourage her with a special treat that showed her how very much He loved her.

This is her testimony of hearing the voice of Jesus:

HILDA: *'I never felt so loved.'*

'Since May 2003, it has been a great blessing to Walter and me to live with our precious only daughter Pearl and our beloved son-in-law Mick.'

'During 2002 I had been very poorly and began to realise that I could no longer care for Walter in our own home. It was a huge worry to us both and despite our daughter arranging for a lovely lady from our church called Lesley to clean our home each week as well as finding us a gardener, Ken, to keep our weeds down, we still struggled. Pearl was in full time work as a technical author and could only manage to pop in on her way home to check if we were alright. Something had to change.'

'That year also, Mick's father (Graham) had suffered a sudden stroke and within 3 months had died of a brain tumour. Mick's family had rallied together wonderfully, providing round-the-clock company and care for him for his 3-month stay in hospital, helping to feed him and wet his lips when he could not swallow, but then when the doctors discharged him to a Care Home, saying that there was nothing else that they could do for him, his care fell apart. One day everyone had to put in an appearance at work, so the Care Home workers were entrusted to provide his essential care needs. By lunchtime when the first family members arrived to see Graham, they were heart-broken to find that his breakfast was still in front of him because no member of staff had bothered to feed him. Nor had anyone bothered to make him comfortable.'

'"*Didn't you want your breakfast, Graham?*" a care worker said sheepishly, poking his head round the door to check on things now that some of the family had arrived. They knew full well that their patient was paralysed and could not feed himself! The tray was whisked from under his nose and a dinner tray plonked in front of him. Meantime his bedding and clothes had not been changed. Things could not have been worse. Immediately there was a family confab and it was decided to take Graham back home where the family could continue to look after him round the clock. Mick's sisters took compassionate leave from their nursing jobs and the others fitted in whenever they could.'

'The following week Mick's sister Sandra 'phoned to say that his father had agreed to be prayed for by a minister. We all knew that the end was near. Graham had managed to mumble, "Mick", and Sandra took it that he would rather have his son Mick pray for him. Then Sandra had a sudden idea and suggested that Pearl's father might come along to pray for him, being a minister. Sandra must have sensed that her father needed some closure with God now that he was facing eternity.'

'It was with great anticipation that Walter and I, accompanied by Mick and Pearl, entered the hushed atmosphere of the living room where Graham was lying on a special hospital-type bed. Sandra welcomed us in and we all gathered around as Graham opened his eyes and smiled weakly in recognition. Walter explained why we had all come together to see him. Graham knew that Mick − and we, as a family − loved and served God, so he nodded that he would like Walter to pray with him.'

'Walter took the opportunity to explain to Graham as clearly as he could that Jesus loved him and died on a cross as a sacrifice so that the barrier of sin between him and God could be forgiven.[30] Walter then asked Graham if he understood what he had said. He nodded with his eyes. Then Walter asked Graham if he would like to accept Jesus as his Saviour. Again, Graham nodded.'

'With great joy in our hearts, we all bowed our heads around the bed as Walter prayed with Graham to ask Jesus to become his Lord and Saviour.' We were so thrilled because up until that point, Graham had shown no interest in Christianity or the message of the cross.'

'It was only after we had left the room that Graham spoke his last words to Mick. He said, "*Mick, are you there?*"

Startled at his father's sudden ability to speak, Mick replied, "*Yes, Dad, I'm here,*" and he quickly walked back to his Dad's bedside.

"*I'm ready to go up now,*" Graham said. This was from a man who was paralysed and had not been able to speak for days! Mick knew then that his Dad had made his peace with God and was ready to meet his Maker.'

---

[30] Hebrews 9:22 'Without the shedding of blood there is no forgiveness of sins.'

'This series of events had a profound effect on my son-in-law. He immediately knew that he could not bear to see any other of our family go into Care. Yet Walter and I were struggling to cope with living in our own home and had been contemplating asking if there was any room for us in Bedford, where we knew there was a Christian Old People's Home. We shed many tears together, as childhood sweethearts, presuming that our lives together were drawing to a close.'

'Very soon after that, events took a swift turn and we found ourselves selling Ivy Cottage, our beloved house in Nottingham, while Mick and Pearl sold theirs. In due course we were whisked away to large 5-bedroomed house in Barlborough near Chesterfield, to enjoy a whole new lease of life with our daughter Pearl caring for us.'

'This is where I heard the voice of Jesus.'

'Life had gone swimmingly for a number of years. We welcomed our friend's regular visits and enjoyed the fellowship of Hope City Church in Sheffield, which we all attended. The Pastor there, David Gilpin, made such a fuss of Walter and me, and he even put our pictures up in the 'Hall of Fame' along the upstairs corridor. Even when I was unable to leave the house and travel to church, I was still able to enjoy the cell group meeting at our house, and various members would visit us, including Pastor David. Those were precious times.'

'Walter and I were even invited to a special banquet held in our honour by the AoG Church in Station Road, Carlton,

Nottingham. It was such a great joy to see all our beloved friends again.'

'That proved to be the last time I left the house unaided. It had been such a struggle to climb the flight of steps at the front of the house on our return late at night, with Walter pulling and Mick pushing me from behind, that I never again dared to venture out except into the rear garden.'

'In order to make my life easier, Pearl arranged a lovely bedroom for me downstairs in Walter's former office, so that I only needed to take a few steps from my bed to reach my comfy chair in our lounge, with all other amenities close at hand. Still, it was hard to endure the discomfort of old age. I remember my father, William Potter, saying that he wouldn't wish it on his worst enemy to reach 90!'

'One long, lonely night when Walter, Mick and Pearl were all tucked up in bed upstairs fast asleep, I began praying, as I so often did, for the family, our friends, and all the missionaries I could think of. There was a gentle golden glow in the room from the salt lamp that Pearl had placed by my bedside.'

'Suddenly a glowing, white figure came through the wall and leant over me, His face close to mine.'

'"*Hilda, love,*" He said, with such tenderness that I immediately knew it was my Lord and Saviour, Jesus Christ. He smiled as I looked up at Him in recognition. Then as suddenly as He had arrived, He left again, passing through the bedroom wall.'

'I was elated beyond the capacity for words to describe. All the sense of loneliness and dejection left me in that moment and my soul was flooded with peace and joy: my Saviour had come to comfort me in my hour of need.'

My Congo Lili

Since returning to Nottingham, Mick and I have made some awesome new friends, particularly through our new connect group, as well as renewing old friendships.

Since I grew up in the Congo, whenever I meet anyone who could possibly be from Africa at Heart Church[31] where we now attend, I always ask where they are from, just in case I might one day be able to speak in Kiluba to them, my own African language.

One day I was told that a young couple from the Congo had joined our church but that they attended the second service. I was hugely curious, so one week I managed to secure an introduction. Sadly, they were from Kinshasa, not from Katanga, so they spoke a different language entirely, called Lingala. Nevertheless, we have bonded so well with them and they are now among our very best friends.

The husband, Sedu, immediately began helping Mick to sort out our huge garden, which was an enormous help. Through him, we

[31] The Pentecostal church on Talbot St., formerly known as The Christian Centre.

got to know his wife, Lili, better and we invited them round for Sunday lunch.

Over the months, I have been able to give them artefacts from the Congo to grace their home and we now attend the same connect group, which is a huge joy to us. At one of these group meetings, Lili happened to mention that she had heard the audible voice of Jesus – in fact, she regularly does, she says.

Sedu and Lili with Pearl and Mick

LILI: *'I regularly hear the voice of Jesus.'*

'I first heard God speak to me in an audible voice when I was 10 years old. The year was 1997. I lived with my family in Mont-

Ngafula and one day as I was in my bedroom, God's voice spoke to me clearly saying, *"Leave everything you do that's not right and follow Me."'*

'It was a Saturday morning and I rushed to tell my Mum what had happened. She told me, *"If you hear the voice again, you should say – Here I am, Lord, use me."'*

'I heard God's voice 3 times in all, saying the same words, *"Leave everything you do that's not right and follow Me."'*

'A year later, I made a commitment at 11 years of age to follow Jesus as my Lord and Saviour. I have been following Him ever since and I know that God has placed a call on my life.'

'Since then, I have heard God's audible voice several times. For example, I knew a notable Congolese musician who was a singer/songwriter of Christian music living in Kinshasa, who used to play the guitar and bless people with his worship songs.'

'By the beginning of August 2013, I was living in Nottingham when I heard God's voice clearly telling me that this Congolese musician had passed away. I was shocked and tried to find out what had happened to him but no one knew anything about it in Kinshasa. All I could do was pray for him, because I knew that God had audibly spoken to me about his death.'

'A day later, the musician actually died and word spread like wildfire. What amazed me was that God had warned me the day before, of his impending death.'

CHAPTER 4: Family Healings

'We prevail with men by impudence because they are displeased
with it, but with God because He is pleased with it.'
MATTHEW HENRY[32]

Grandma's Polypus

I could fill a book just by describing the healings experienced by my close family members, let alone all the many healings of friends and acquaintances. One such healing comes to mind when my Grandma Hawkins had a polypus at the back of her nose in 1932. My father starts the story:

WALTER: *'I was there with my mother when it happened.'*

'I was about 14 years old and had just left school when my mother began to experience acute difficulties in breathing and swallowing her food. Very soon she couldn't even lie down at night but had to be propped up in bed in order to be able to breathe at all. She was constantly choking and as a young lad I found this very frightening. Many were the times that I could hear her almost suffocating and crying out for help in the night.'

---

[32] British Nonconformist minister, best known for his six-volume biblical commentary *Exposition of the Old and New Testaments* (1706).

Walter with his mother Lottie and father Walter Hawkins (Snr)
in 1934

'In the end, my father could stand it no longer and despite my mother's remonstrations he insisted that she should get the doctor to look at her throat. After a brief examination the doctor found that her nose was blocked on both sides and that a lump was obstructing the back of her throat. He immediately sent her to the Chesterfield Royal hospital, which was then located in the middle of the town.'

'No one from our church dared go to the hospital in those days because everyone was encouraged to exercise their faith, so it was with a great sense of shame that my mother caught the bus into Chesterfield on the day of the appointment. She felt as if she was letting the standard down!'

'Her examination by the ear, nose and throat specialist must have been very gruelling because it caused mother to haemorrhage badly and she almost choked to death. She was immediately scheduled for an operation the following Monday.'

'I recall how upset mother was when she returned from the hospital. She wept in my father's arms and asked him what she should do. She really didn't want to let go of her faith that God could heal her. Father simply said, "*We're praying for you to be healed.*" He could do no more.'

'That night while father and I were sleeping, God spoke to mother that the root of the matter was dead and she felt a real peace come over her. Straight away in the morning, she wrote to cancel the operation. Meanwhile, we all continued to pray intensely for her healing.'

'The following Friday when I came home from work, mother was seated in the chair facing the kitchen sink. Suddenly she cried out, "*Oh, oh, oooh,*" and leapt over to the sink holding her hands to her face. I turned just in time to witness a dark red mass emerging from each nostril until it was dangling like two long sausages from her nose. Then she began to choke as the polypus started to bulge out of her mouth like an expanding balloon. She couldn't breathe at all. I felt so helpless; all I could do was run to the sink and hold her. By now a gargantuan, loathsome mass was protruding from each orifice until her features were almost obliterated by it. Still my mother was choking, totally unable to breathe. I could sense her struggling to expel the thing, rasping, gagging violently until she had expelled the last bit of air from her lungs.'

'I was horrified. I thought that my mother was going to die in my arms.'

'In her abject panic, mother tossed her head back and suddenly the dark red sausages slid back into her nostrils and the entire polypus fell down into the back of her throat and came away through her mouth in one complete mass. It landed in the sink like a stinking, quivering jelly. Free of the obstruction at last, mother noisily sucked in a grateful gulp of air, her body trembling with a sudden overwhelming weakness and she fell back into my arms. *"Son,"* she cried, *"I've been healed!"'*

'Once the polypus came away, that was the end of it. The moment God had said to mother that the root of the matter was dead, He touched it and the polypus died. Thank God it never returned throughout the remainder of her 86 years. She had a complete and perfect healing.'

LOTTIE: *'I determined to trust the Lord.'*

'My husband, Walter, and I had been attending the Pentecostal church in North Wingfield for several years since it opened in December 1925. It was a very exciting phase of our lives because this was during the time when the Jeffreys brothers were touring around the country holding healing meetings. Naturally there was a lot of talk within the church about all the healings that were taking place and this encouraged us all to believe in God for our own healing and good health.'

'Walter had recently been elected as an elder of the church when I began to notice that something was growing in the back of my nose and down into my throat. The growth seemed to enlarge quite rapidly until I could no longer breathe normally through my nose. It reached a stage where I could hardly swallow and I was forced to eat only soft foods for fear of choking. I asked for prayer at the church and we all began to trust God that He would heal me. My symptoms became so bad that eventually my husband told me to see the doctor. At first I declined, thinking that this would show a distinct lack of faith on my part but then Walter persuaded me that we should at least find out what the problem was so that we would know better how to pray.'

'My doctor immediately referred me to the Chesterfield Royal hospital to see an ear, nose and throat specialist. When I got to the hospital the consultant stretched me out on a couch but since I couldn't breathe lain down, I began to choke badly and he had to sit me back up again quickly. Once I had regained my breath, he began inserting various tools up my nose and into my mouth to find out what was causing the obstruction. He found that my nose was completely sealed at the back and that I couldn't breathe through it at all. The examination suddenly terminated when blood began pouring profusely out of my nostrils and also down the back of my throat. I was in such a state that the consultant had to call for help to get the situation under control. For a moment I thought I was going to die. There was blood everywhere and I simply could not catch my breath, so much blood was trickling down the back of my throat into my lungs. I was really frightened by the experience.'

'The eventual verdict was that I had a large polypus growing into my sinuses and down the back of my throat, completely blocking the passage of air through my nostrils. I was summarily booked for an operation to take place the following week. At the time, I was so shaken by the examination and everything seemed to happen so quickly around me that I was given no opportunity to decline the surgery.'

'When I returned home I was very distressed because I felt as if I had betrayed everyone; my husband as the elder of the church, the pastor, my fellow church members and most of all, the Lord. I dreaded telling anyone about what had happened. That night I was earnestly seeking God as to what to do about the forthcoming operation. I couldn't sleep. Suddenly, I felt a warm sensation come over me and I felt the Lord tell me very clearly, *"The root of the matter is dead."'*

'Immediately, I woke my husband up and told him, *"Walter, God has told me that the root of the matter is dead, so if it's dead it can't get any worse, and so I'm trusting God for it. I'm not going to have that operation.'* A real sense of peace came over me then and at last I was able to get a little rest.'

'Early the next morning, I wrote a letter to the consultant who had arranged the operation saying, *"Thank you for all you thought to do for me, but as I am a believer in divine healing, I have decided to trust the Lord."* It was a simple act of faith but it meant a great deal to me. Without God's divine intervention the outcome for my health could have been extremely serious, as continued growth of the polypus at its former rate would have led quite rapidly to total obstruction of my airways. There was a real risk that I could choke to death.'

'Meantime nothing seemed to have changed outwardly. My breathing was just as laboured as before and I still couldn't swallow my food. I had not had a decent night's sleep for weeks because I had to sit propped up in my bed with as many pillows as I could find.'

'That Friday afternoon, just as my son Walter was coming through the back door, I suddenly began to choke. I ran to the sink because I thought that I had a nose bleed, then I realised that something was dangling from my nose. I tried to blow through my blocked nostrils but it seemed as if there was a huge congealed mass in there and it was obviously far too bulky to expel through my nose. The next thing I knew, a massive blob tasting of blood was coming down the back of my throat and into my mouth. It was an awful, frightening experience. I realised that it must be something to do with the polypus but I had never imagined just how extensive the growth was. It filled my nostrils; it filled the back of my throat; it filled my mouth. It seemed to be everywhere! I just couldn't breathe no matter how hard I tried to get rid of the thing.'

'Finally, I managed to cough the entire polypus out through my mouth and it came away in one mass and fell into the sink. The bleeding quickly stopped and I was soon able to breathe normally again through my nostrils. I was so happy; I couldn't stop praising the Lord! That night, I was able to lie down in the bed and sleep properly for the first time in a long while.'

'On Sunday at church, I sat in my usual seat at the front, 2nd seat in next to my husband and I couldn't wait to give my testimony of how God had completely healed me. The whole congregation was thrilled with excitement. I think that word of my healing had got around before ever I stood up to speak but still they all wanted to hear every detail from my own lips. Some even wanted to peer into my mouth and see for themselves after the meeting ended! It was a great boost to us all.'

'The following week it was such a joy to me to be able to return to the consultant for an examination and to hear him confirm that it was a miracle; the polypus had gone without a trace. He did warn me, however, that these things can often grow back again. Thank God that in my case it was a perfect healing. Despite the consultant's fears, the polypus never recurred!'

'In those days when evangelists such as Stephen Jeffreys were touring Britain holding healing campaigns, to have a miraculous healing occur in our local assembly without the laying on of hands by any of the great preachers encouraged everyone in the church to believe God for themselves. It also inspired our new young pastor Wilfred Colliss to step out in faith and pray for the sick in our meetings. That is when Joan Taylor and others in our assembly were healed.'

'When God Himself touches your body and heals you, you are never the same again. You know, because you know deep in your soul, that He is real and that He answers prayer.'

Grandad's Back

Walter and Lottie Hawkins in 1949

My Grandad Hawkins stood 6' 1" tall, a handsome 14-stone giant of a man. His hands were so massive they could fit around my

Grandma's waist and then some! Grandma first saw Grandad when he was being carried off a local football pitch by the team members on their shoulders for having scored the winning goal! First and foremost though, he was an athlete, taking part in track events as a sprint runner in the 100-yard dash when, at his best, he was only half a second behind the world record of his day.

Grandma was already a powerful preacher when they met; she had been on the Methodist circuit since the age of 17 years.

Grandad was not yet a Christian.

Three months after their wedding, they had their first big argument. It must have been a humdinger because Grandad lashed out and whacked Grandma across the left cheek.

Stunned, she ran upstairs and fell onto her knees by her bedside.

"What shall I do, Lord?" she sobbed. *"If he's treating me like this after only 3 months of being married, what will he be like later on?"*

The answer came when she opened her Bible. The page amazingly fell open at these words: "... *but whosoever shall smite thee on thy right cheek, turn to him the other also.*"[33] Drying her eyes, she returned downstairs to a hard-faced glare from her husband.

---

[33] Matthew 5:39, KJV

"Walter," she said softly, *"My Bible tells me that if he strikes thee on the one cheek, to offer him the other cheek also."* Quietly, she approached him and turned her right cheek towards him. *"Here it is,"* she pointed. *"Strike this one too."*

Grandad visibly crumpled and took her in his arms, all his anger dissipated. This was the turning point for him and soon afterwards he knelt beside her and asked God to forgive him of his sins. Thus began a remarkable journey for Grandad that led him from being an illiterate sportsman to being an elder and ultimately the pastor of North Wingfield AoG church in Derbyshire for many years. During that time Grandma taught him not only to trust in God but also to read and write.

This is Grandad's testimony of how God healed his back:

WALTER HAWKINS SENIOR: *'I knew if I could only get to the church, I'd be healed.'*

'I was working on the coal face at Williamthorpe Colliery in Holmewood, Chesterfield when my accident happened. The year was 1928. As always it had been an incredibly hard shift starting at 6 o'clock in the morning and I was worn out by the end of a long day shovelling coal. My face and hands were black and my clothes stuck to my body with all the sweating I had done down the pit. I couldn't wait to get home to a hot meal and a bath so I ran to collect my bicycle and started off down the hill at a fair old rate.'

'In those days I lived on Chesterfield Road in North Wingfield, which was about half an hour's journey away. Coming down Temple Normanton Hill was always tricky as the road was very steep and it was sometimes hard to control your speed, especially if it was wet or the brakes were slipping. At the bottom of the hill were two ponds, one on either side of the road. Whenever it rained, the two ponds would meet across the road in a pool. People would have to wade through all this water and sometimes it became impassable for vehicles. Over the years, gullies had formed in the hollow that were hard to negotiate when you were riding a bike.'

'I had just reached the bottom when I hit one of these ruts. I catapulted straight over the handle bars and landed like a lead weight on my back, skidding along the gravely road surface with my bike tangled in my legs. Shooting pains darted up my spine and for a moment I dare not move. I was stunned and smarting from my wounds, lying spread-eagled in the road.'

'The person cycling behind me nearly collided with me and I remember feeling foolish and annoyed with myself for having fallen right in front of the other miners who were dodging past me on all sides, trying not to crash into me or my mangled bike. I would be the talk of the pit on the next shift and would doubtless have to take some hefty stick from all the lads for weeks on end, I thought, groaning inwardly.'

'By now my head was spinning. I was conscious of cycle bells sounding out a warning to the others coming down the hill. Wheels were whizzing past my head at breakneck speed and I realised I was in danger of being run over if I stayed in the middle of the road so I made an effort to pick myself up. It was then I found that I couldn't move.'

'The miners who had followed me down the hill pulled up as soon as they saw me fall. A few of the lads ran over to me and tried to pick me up but I yelled out in pain. They immediately called for someone to ride back up to the pit and fetch the colliery ambulance. Others were directing traffic around me. They all said I was very fortunate not to have landed on my head or I could have been maimed for life or even killed.'

'Within minutes, I found myself on the way to Chesterfield Royal Hospital. The pain was unbearable and I felt every bump along the way. When we arrived, I was so badly caked in muck and coal dust that I was soiling everything I touched, so the nurses had to clean me up before ever the doctors could take a look at me. Eventually I was examined all over. They were pulling and prodding, bending my knees and neck until I screamed out in pain. My, did it hurt! But thank God they found no broken bones.'

'I was a strong lad, they said. I suppose they were right in them days; I'd done a lot of running and playing football in my time. But I was over 6 feet tall and it was a very heavy tumble I'd taken off that bike. Something had ripped inside my back because I couldn't walk or lift myself up and I was in agony even when I lay perfectly still. They didn't have all them new-fangled machines to look inside you back then, so all they could do was patch up my external wounds. The consultant told me that I would need complete bed rest for several weeks, then they would see how I was getting on. That was all they could offer me; pain killers and bed rest. He hoped that eventually the swelling would subside and that one day I would get back on my feet again.'

'I didn't want to stay for weeks on end in the hospital so the consultant agreed that I could go home and lie in my own bed with my wife and doctor to care for me. I was under strict instructions to lie flat on my back and not to move around — *"as if I could do any other!"* I thought sadly. The ambulance men would take me home on a stretcher and make sure that I was comfortable.'

'At home Lottie, my wife, had been worried sick about me. I hadn't turned up for dinner and she always made sure that a piping hot meal was waiting for me when I returned from work each day. She quickly made up a makeshift bed for me on our old sofa in the sitting room so that she wouldn't have to keep going up and down stairs to see to me. I don't think they could have lifted me up that narrow staircase anyway! The sofa was one of those old-type settees with a scroll end on each arm. I was so tall that my head had to lean over one arm, supported by pillows, with my feet dangling over the other end. It was incredibly uncomfortable but at least I was home.'

'Lottie fed me something to eat and prayed with me. She was a good woman, was my Lottie. Then it was time to get ready for church. I was the elder and we always went to every meeting; my wife, my young son and I. Walter was 10 years old at the time and already called to be a missionary to the Congo. I was determined to get there even after all that had happened; even though I couldn't walk. In all those years that I had been a Christian, I had never missed a meeting — never been late, even. I could not countenance missing the meeting that night because I knew in my heart that if only somehow I could get there, I would be healed.'

'The trouble was that nobody in our church owned a car. We didn't even have telephones in those days. There was no one to help me but the Lord; I had to put my trust in Him alone. But I was determined to go as if my very life depended on it, so I told Lottie to dress me and fetch my coat. We were both firm believers in divine healing so she knew what I was about to do. I began to inch my legs off the sofa. Even sitting up for her to put my clothes on was a challenge. I leaned forward and managed to slip my feet into my shoes, and then she tied the laces for me. Lottie was looking very dubious but she could see the look in my eyes that said I would not take "*no*" for an answer.'

''Time was ticking by. It took an enormous struggle for me to drag myself to my feet, pulling myself up bit by bit using any support within reach. Lottie and my young son could give me no help as neither was able to bear my weight. The pain was so terribly excruciating that I had to grit my teeth so as not to let them know how much agony I was in. I could not stand up straight but at least I was on my feet at last. I took several breaths, steadied myself and then with an enormous effort shuffled one foot forward, holding tightly onto the mantle piece. After another few breaths I dragged the other leg to join it. I could so easily have toppled back onto the sofa and given up at that point but defeat was not a possibility for me. I had to get to that meeting. I had to be healed.'

'At that instant I knew just how the woman with the issue of blood felt in the Bible, when she said, "*If I may but touch his garment, I shall be whole.*"[34] That's what I wanted. There was so much at stake. I had to be able to go to work; we needed my wages to be able to pay the bills and buy food. There was not as much help around in those days if you fell upon hard times. You just had to make the most of life and get on with things, regardless of the cost and regardless of the pain.'

'Step by step, slowly I inched towards the door. Getting over the doorstep was another hurdle to face and then I began creeping slowly down the alley, supporting myself along the walls, with Lottie and Walter following on behind. At each step I had to will myself to go on. Finally, we reached the street. I was breathing heavily, almost in a state of collapse.'

'It was only a 5-minute walk to our church normally, yet that night it had taken me at least 10 minutes just to reach the end of our row. At this rate we would be late even though we had started out extra early. I looked up the street at the long rows of terraced houses lining Chesterfield Road and my heart sank — but I just had to go

---

[34] Matthew 9:21, KJV

on, clinging to every wall and gate that would support my weight along the route. My progress was pitifully slow and I was in more agony than I could ever have imagined.'

'When we reached Lings Row, I grabbed the boundary wall and crawled my way along it with my arms, dragging my feet behind as I went. Young Walter could bear this no longer and ran on ahead to alert the folks at the church of my predicament. He hoped to be able to get someone strong enough to help. By the time I reached the railway crossings, the brethren had come out to meet me. Was I glad to see them! They almost carried me up the steps into the church.'

'The meeting had started already when they dragged me in and took me straight up to the front for prayer. A.C. Colliss stopped the hymn singing and straightway came over to me. I briefly told him what had happened and that I knew that if only I could get to the church, I would be healed. A.C. told the church that I had been a very courageous man and it hurt him so to see me in such agony. He laid his hands on my back and simply asked God to heal me. By faith I stood to full height; the pain was gone.'

'That night I walked home marvellously healed. It was a miracle.'

WALTER: *'He was straight as a ramrod.'*

'I was only 10 years old when I saw my Dad healed. These things were real. I saw Dad lying helpless on the settee, unable to walk. Then Mam prayed for him; he was in such agony. I saw Dad pull himself off the settee and drag himself inch by inch out of the house and along the walls. His face was grey and he was in such pain I couldn't bear to look at him.'

'I ran ahead to the church to warn them that Dad was on his way, crawling and dragging himself along the street in terrible pain. I told them what he had said about being healed if only he could just get to church for prayer. Mam stopped with him all the way.'

'When they brought Dad in he was bowed over and shaking. He could not stand without support. We were singing a hymn but Pastor A.C. Collis stopped the meeting immediately to pray for him. I was standing right by my Dad and I saw him straighten up like a ramrod when God healed him. The colour returned to his cheeks and I could see that the pain had gone.'

'Two days later he was back at work, crawling on his hands and knees to the coal face and digging and shovelling coal all day long in those cramped conditions. The doctors could not believe it was possible. But with God, anything is possible. It was a real miracle and I witnessed it happen.'

Mum's Migraine

Some of the enduring memories for me as a youngster were my mother's bouts of illness. We always used to laugh at the time that my Grandad Potter was a 'creaking gate' but looking back, my mother also has tended to suffer all sorts of niggling health problems. During our stay in Sunderland where my father was pastor of the Assembly of God church between 1960 and 1963, Mum seemed to be regularly holed up in her bedroom with the curtains drawn. At the time, I couldn't understand why Dad was always holding his finger over his lips and telling me to 'shush'. He and I used to creep about the house for days whilst my mother lay in agony upstairs. It's then that we found out that Mum was suffering from migraine attacks. I had never heard of anything like it. Being a healthy child, I had no concept of what a headache must be like but then my mother's days of agony were a startling wake up call to me and pain became a part of our daily routine.

So, life went on until the day we went to Ryhope Assembly to hear an evangelist called Richard Bolt preaching. It must have been the hottest day of the year; I have never, ever been so full-on baked except perhaps in a sauna. People were wafting their hymn sheets furiously and the stench of freely flowing body odour made me want to gag, especially when we started to sing some choruses and everybody began clapping their hands and waving their arms in the air! Salty perspiration was streaming down my forehead into my eyes and down my nose into my mouth. My hankie was soaking wet and still it got hotter and hotter. Suddenly, I began coughing uncontrollably as a persistent tickle grabbed my throat and being a shy 11-year old I went beetroot colour with the sheer embarrassment of it all.

They tried opening all the windows but it was like the sirocco wind fanning a blazing furnace inside the cramped room. A chorus of dry coughing ensued. Then the door at the back was opened wide but still the place felt airless. Those were the hottest two hours of my life in more ways than one, because in this most unlikely hovel of a chapel, on this hottest of days, in that unhealthiest of environments and sweltering heat, my mother was healed of her migraine attacks. This is her story:

HILDA: *'I remember him pointing at me.'*

'During the early '60s my husband Walter and I were extremely busy as pastor and wife of the Sunderland Assembly in County Durham, England. We had taken the pastorate after our return from the Congo in 1960 as missionary refugees. We had lost everything we owned in Africa due to the violent uprisings in the Congo and it was tough getting started again. Generous friends and family helped us by giving us their spare furniture and bedding but still there were many things we lacked. Walter, Pearl and I were obliged to share just one orange or apple a week between us; no chance of 5 fruit or vegetable portions per person in those days!'

'Apart from convening the eight weekly services held at our own church and visiting sick church members it was customary for us to support any of the local assemblies whenever they held conventions or special meetings. So, when a well-known healing evangelist called Richard Bolt came to speak at Ryhope, of course we were glad to be there. I had been having a lot of migraine headaches and I even had one during that meeting but I never once thought of going forward for healing myself because we were too busy praying for others from our own congregation who had gone along to be prayed for.'

'The time came for Richard to speak but after a few minutes he stopped and pointed straight at me. I was sitting eight rows back, four or five seats in to the left of the aisle. When a finger points right at you, it's like someone pointing a gun; it makes you sit up. He said, "*You have pain behind the eyes and in your head.*" I froze for a moment, my heart pounding. Could he possibly mean me? It was a precise description of how I was feeling.'

'"*The lady sitting back there ...*" He pointed with his finger. Still I didn't respond; I seemed frozen to my seat. The evangelist began counting the rows back and said, "*You're in the eighth row back – you're in that row there.*" Again, he began motioning with his hand. I looked left and right to make sure that no one else in my row had responded, but I knew in my heart that he had pointed his finger at me. Finally, I looked straight at him. "*Yes, you,*" he assured me.'

'So, I shuffled along the row and went out for prayer. Just a simple prayer and a hand lain on my head yet my life was transformed after that. I continued in faith that the migraines wouldn't come back – and praise God, they didn't!'

The Growth on Mum's Leg

In 1971, an irregular-shaped dark brown blotch appeared on the skin of Mum's right leg. At first, she didn't notice the blemish because it was tucked away about 4 inches below the back of the knee towards the outer side on the fattest part of the calf. Since Mum has never been very flexible or athletic, this is a part of her body she rarely, if ever, caught sight of and it is possible that the growth may have remained undetected for some weeks.

As summer approached, Mum's calf began itching. At first, she put it down to the heat and assumed that she must have developed a heat rash, or else had been bitten by an insect, because she could feel a raised area on the back of her leg. Then Dad and I noticed the dark patch on her leg. At first, we passed it off as one of the many large black freckles that we had all accumulated from sun damage incurred during the years we had spent in the Congo (sun screen was a luxury we could not afford in those days). But then later we realised that the patch was growing quite rapidly and that it was taking on an irregular, crusty appearance. Worse still, another dark blotch was beginning to appear next to it. The growth was spreading and beginning to look rather nasty.

Mum looked quite worried when we pointed the blotches out to her and she made an appointment to see her doctor the next day.

"*I think we had better let a specialist look at this,*" the doctor told her. "*It will need removing as quickly as possible. I'll make an appointment for you at the local hospital straight away.*"

"*Well, I'm going on holiday next week,*" Mum interjected, not wanting to miss out on her precious moments by the sea. "*So please could you make the appointment for after I get back?*"

"It's up to you," the doctor replied dubiously. He obviously felt that time was of the essence in this case. He was suspecting a potentially life-threatening malignant melanoma.

HILDA: *'My friend just happened to notice the growth on my leg as I was walking in front of her.'*

'In the summer of 1971, my husband, Walter, and I joined as usual with our friends Cathy and David for a holiday on the south coast in Chard, Devonshire. It was our custom to stay with my long-time friend, Evelyn Oxborrow, who happened to live in a quaint cottage in Chard and so it was a good opportunity for me to enjoy her company during our holiday each year. Walter had brought along his painting easel and David was keen to explore the coves and cliff-top walks along the coast. Surrounded by such beautiful scenery in the company of our great friends, I tried to put to one side any anxious thoughts about the growths on the back of my leg. In fact, I never mentioned them to anyone for fear of putting a dampener on our weeklong getaway.'

'I first met Evelyn in 1941 when we were both nursing at Willersley Castle in Derbyshire during the war years. The castle had been turned into a maternity unit for the surrounding cities in the hope that it would provide a safe haven for the expectant mothers to protect them from any potential bombings. There had been quite a few of us Christians billeted at the castle including several prospective missionaries like myself, so we became a happy crowd, holding prayer meetings in our spare time and building up life-long friendships. It was there at Willersley, in the private chapel by the Derwent River, that Walter proposed to me in June 1942, so those were especially happy times for me — by the way, I said *"Yes,"* of course to Walter's proposal and so I left Willersley at the end of 1943 to marry Walter on 15th January 1944.'

'Whenever we went on holiday to Chard we would attend the local AoG Church and it was there that we met up with George and Hilda Deakin, who were AoG ministers and good friends of Evelyn Oxborrow. We all arranged to meet up on the beach the next day and it was while I happened to be walking barefooted on the sands in front of Hilda that she suddenly spotted the brown growths on my calf.'

"'I don't like the look of those marks on your leg, Hilda," she said, pointing to the back of my right leg.'

'Of course, the story was out then and everybody was very concerned for me. With no more ado, Hilda Deakin laid hands on the growths there and then on the sands in front of everybody sunbathing on the beach, and prayed for God's healing power to come upon me. I was very grateful for her concern and pleased that she prayed for me. At the same time, I was rather embarrassed that my friends had found out about my predicament, along with a beach-load of curious onlookers!'

'A couple of days after we returned home at the end of the week, I woke up to find dry crusts of the growth in my bed. It looked as if a top layer had come off, like a layer of sunburnt skin might peel away. I quickly scooped the pieces up into an envelope to show my doctor the next day and then hurriedly dressed before rushing downstairs to make breakfast.'

'Later when I returned upstairs to make the bed, I found a horrible, dried up black object between the sheets, about an inch in diameter with 2" strands hanging underneath. It looked like a miniature man-o-war jelly fish with long black tentacles dangling from it. I immediately inspected my leg and found that the skin had returned to normal — not even a scar remained where the tentacles had been!'

'What a miracle! I couldn't wait to show my doctor the next day. He had been very anxious to measure the rate of growth of this suspected malignancy after my holiday and an appointment had already been made for me at the surgery, along with another at the hospital for a biopsy.'

'After inspecting my leg, I gathered the pieces of the growth together and examined them carefully. It seemed to me by the way the two main segments fitted together that the two growths on my leg had been partially growing into one other, with one dipping down under the other in a second layer or fold. The smaller secondary growth had much shorter, thinner tentacles than the large man-o-war.'

'The following day when I presented the dried crusts to my doctor, he was amazed and was even more impressed when I told him what had happened on the beach. He insisted that I should keep the hospital appointment as arranged.'

'"*I think you'd better take these to the hospital and show them to the consultant there*," he said, handing the desiccated growths back to me. "*He will be very interested to see what has happened.*"'

'Well, as it happened, the people at the hospital were not at all impressed because I no longer had anything for them to treat!'

'Ever since 1971, the growth has never returned, not in that spot nor anywhere else on my body. Praise God! I was completely and permanently healed!'

Mick's Neck

My husband Mick has had a problem with his neck, on and off, for years. Not every healing is straight forward and simple; not every prayer answered positively. Sometimes God says, "*Wait ... I'm doing something different with you this time.*"

MICK: '*I heard him say that God wanted to heal someone with a neck injury.*'

'When I was 14 years old, I had a very serious bike accident. My friend and I were racing down the steepest part of Woodthorpe Avenue in Mapperley, Nottingham when the back axle of my bicycle broke and I was catapulted off the bike at breakneck speed, narrowly missing a lamp post and a tree trunk before I landed in a heap on the pavement. I was barely conscious but before passing out, I remember thinking, *"This is it. I'm dead."'*

'At the hospital, the staff missed the fact that my spine had cracked between vertebrae 5 and 6. This was only discovered years later by X-ray. I could not lift my head but they sent me home without even a neck brace for support. I lay on the sofa unable to move for several days. Eventually, I made a reasonable recovery and would have thought no more of the incident but for the pain in my neck that increased steadily as the years progressed.'

'By the time I met my wife Pearl, this pain was more or less constant. There were times when I could have wrenched my head off, the agony was so severe. No amount of painkillers would touch the spot and massage only brought temporary relief. Before I became a Christian, I would simply drink myself into a stupor in an attempt to deaden the pain but then I met Pearl who introduced me to Jesus and bit by bit my former life changed.'

'However, the pain in my neck was still there. I used to beg God to heal me but nothing happened. After two years there was a special meeting in the Royal Concert Hall in Nottingham where Tim Hall from Australia was the speaker. At the end of his message he began giving prophetic words about different people whom he believed God wanted to heal. I wasn't thinking about my own problem until suddenly he said, *"There are 7 people here with whiplash and other neck injuries. God wants to heal you all."'*

'Pearl prodded me in the back and after some hesitation I raised my hand along with 6 others. No one prayed specifically for me or laid hands on me but from that instant I began to feel different. I could feel a warmth coursing down my arms and I began praising God in an unknown language. It was a life-defining experience and I walked out of that building without any pain.'

'The neck pain did not return for at least two years after that but as I was accustomed to lifting heavy boxes in my job, further injuries would occur from time to time and eventually I found myself in as much agony as before.'

'One morning, I was walking up Porchester Road in Nottingham on my way to work, praying as I went along the route as usual. This was my opportunity to touch base with God each day. On this particular occasion, I was in horrendous agony and I remember just saying to the Lord, "*God, you've done it before. Do it again.*" My prayer was as simple and direct as that. Immediately my pain left me and I reached work a new man.'

'My healing has been an ongoing saga. A few years later a massively heavy crate fell from a palate off a lorry right onto my head. My neck was compressed and back came the familiar agonising pain. I tried all sorts of remedies from visiting the chiropractor and physiotherapist, and trying various manipulations and stretching techniques but to no real avail. Sometimes I would say to God, "*You did it for me before on Porchester Road. Please heal me again now.*"'

'I waited for years for another touch from God. In desperation I tried various specialists, chiropractors and physiotherapists but nothing seemed to help.'

'Then one evening in the summer of 2007 we invited a couple of friends, Steve and George, round for a curry: Steve because he was going to show my wife, Pearl, how to cook an authentic Indian curry; George because his wife, Marilyn, had just returned to their home in Spain leaving George to complete a few jobs in Sheffield before joining her. We chatted after the sumptuous meal as you do and eventually the conversation inevitably turned to Jesus and what He has done for each of us. Steve happened to mention that the Lord had been blessing him recently with a healing ministry. I jumped at this unexpected chance to be prayed for.'

'"*Perhaps you could pray for my neck to be healed, Steve – if you would,*" I asked hopefully.'

'"*Yes, of course!*" he said. "*But I want George to pray and I'll just lay my hands on you.*"'

'I was a little surprised but just happy to have anyone to pray for my neck to be healed. If you know my friend George, he's a real cockney lad. He used to be a market trader and if Jesus hadn't saved him and changed his life, you'd have had to watch your pocket with him around! Instead he is now one of God's real gems.'

'"*God, you know I love my mate Mick,*" George prayed. "*I want You to heal him.*"'

'That was it. Such a simple, direct prayer – but I began to feel different. I could sense God's power in the room.'

'"Now you must trust God," explained Steve. "Every morning when you wake up, thank God for healing you."'

'It seemed such a simple prayer but the principle was profound. It just required faith. Each morning since then, I have thanked God that He is my Healer and I'm happy to be able to report that the grinding pain has gone. If ever I get the even slightest twinge, I just put my hand on my neck and thank God for healing me. As the weeks go by, I am increasingly aware that God has done it again for me. I'm healed!'

CHAPTER 5: Friends' Healings

'Sin and sickness have passed from me to Calvary – salvation and health have passed from Calvary to me.' F.F. BOSWORTH[35]

A bulletin board in the Mayo Clinic in the USA reads, "*Cancer is limited: it cannot cripple love, it cannot shatter hope, it cannot erode faith, it cannot eat away peace, it cannot destroy confidence, it cannot kill friendship, it cannot shut out memories, it cannot silence courage, it cannot invade the soul, it cannot reduce eternal life, it cannot quench the spirit, and it cannot lessen the power of the resurrection.*"

"*It cannot erode faith*". That is a powerful statement. Most people's reactions when told that they have a terminal or life-threatening illness is one of disbelief, quickly followed by intense fear, sorrow and even anger as the realisation dawns that they may not have long to live. Then one has a choice – acceptance of the inevitable or a deep desire to see the prognosis change. It's at this point that faith can take hold and pave the path for a miracle.

---

[35] Fred Francis Bosworth was a healing evangelist and founding member of the Assemblies of God in the USA in 1914; he is best known for his seminal work, 'Christ the Healer', which went through seven editions in his own lifetime.

Arthur's Tuberculosis

Arthur C. Colliss, or A.C. as he was fondly known by my father and all his friends, started his working life as a farmer on Mill Farm, Grassmoor in Derbyshire. He was a giant of a man physically, with a large black moustache and a strong, dominant character. He lived his life by strict moral rules and was fearless in telling the truth as he saw it, yet those who new A.C. well learned to love the gentler side of his character and admired him as a great man of God.

As a young man he was blessed with a powerful voice and became the choir master at a local Methodist church until a very serious illness caused him to go to Scarborough on the Lincolnshire coast in search of medical help and the benefits of sea air. There he was diagnosed with an advanced case of tuberculosis. The story of his healing is taken up by Wesley Beardsmore, a close family friend and retired AoG missionary from the Kalembelembe Field in the former Belgian Congo.

WESLEY. *'He was as fit as a fiddle!'*

'A.C. Colliss was wheeled onto the famous marine drive in Scarborough in a dying condition. He had been coughing up blood profusely and could hardly breathe. In desperation, he started crying to God for help and there in his wheelchair he experienced a miraculous healing and an infilling of the Holy Spirit, which completely transformed his life and gave him a determination to spread the fourfold gospel of Jesus Christ as the Saviour, Healer, Baptiser and Coming King.'

'Back home, this message was not acceptable to his local church and he felt obliged to commence some meetings on his own farm. He began by telling any folks who cared to join him all about his own conversion and healing and then he soon found that people were asking him to pray for their illnesses and bringing their sick friends along to be prayed for as well. Thus, began a significant evangelistic and healing ministry for A.C. Colliss, which eventually resulted in the opening of a new Pentecostal church in the adjacent village of North Wingfield on December 26th 1925, with himself as its first pastor.'

'Three years later, he felt urged by God to take the gospel message to the larger town of Alfreton. At about that time, the original Roman Catholic Church building in Park Street became vacant when a new one was built on the main Nottingham Road. The old church was bought by a local joiner and builder, Mr W.J. Whysall, with the intention of using it as a store and workshop, but before he could change the building in any way, he was approached by Pastor Colliss with a request that he be allowed to conduct a series of evangelistic meetings in it. This short series of revival meetings continued on and on, so much so that the building was never used as a workshop and in fact Mr. & Mrs. Whysall were among the first converts, becoming faithful members and benefactors of the new assembly. That is how the AoG church started in Alfreton in November 1928.'

'My own father, John Thomas Beardsmore, had come from Lower Gornal in Staffordshire to find work in the Alfreton colliery in 1922, bringing the extended family with him. They had been active members of the Lake Street Primitive Methodist Church in Lower Gornal but had never fully integrated into the local congregation. As soon as the revival meetings began in Park Street, most of the group from Staffordshire were attracted to them and soon became members. In fact, the first-time dad went into the Park Street church in December 1928, Pastor Colliss told him afterwards that he had a witness in his spirit that my father would be his helper and right hand man. Almost immediately, my father was appointed as the first elder of the assembly.'

'I was only a child at the time, about 8 years of age, but I remember A.C. Colliss telling us all about how God had healed him on the sea front at Scarborough from tuberculosis. I was fascinated. Most people I knew of in those days who contracted tuberculosis ended up dead sooner or later. It was a dreaded killer disease - but A.C. Colliss was there standing in front of us all, as fit as a fiddle.'

Hannah's St. Vitus Dance

Hannah Buckley

Hannah Buckley became a very good friend of my mother's after she began to attend the neighbouring Alfreton Assembly in Derbyshire from the age of 10 years. Hannah later married Wesley Beardsmore, my father's all-time best friend and both couples later became missionaries to the Congo in Africa. Their lives have run in parallel ever since and they are still ringing each other up even now as I am typing these words, praying for one another's ailments and encouraging each other along life's way, though they are all now in their 90's.

This is the story of Hannah's remarkable healing from St. Vitus Dance:

WESLEY: *'She was her daddy's darling.'*

'Hannah's parents, David and Hannah Buckley, moved from Cromford to Alfreton in Derbyshire with their large family of 9 sons and just one precious daughter Hannah, who was born in 1918. David Buckley was hoping to find work in the colliery to support his burgeoning family. He had once been a local preacher but he and his wife had not been attending church for a while, possibly due to the burden of bringing up so many children during those difficult years of the post war depression. One thing was certain though; David Buckley doted on his little girl.'

'In 1928, aged 10, Hannah was taken very ill and was off school for a full 12 months. She was eventually diagnosed with St. Vitus Dance and Rheumatic Fever. By the end of 1928, the family doctor, Raymond Bingham, anxiously called in a specialist to examine Hannah, whose condition was deteriorating rapidly. The specialist informed Hannah's parents that there was nothing more that medical science could do for their young daughter. They should expect her to die at any time.'

'David and Hannah Buckley tearfully waited for the end of their only daughter's short life, which thus far had been such a joy to her father. They were fully expecting the worst but hoping desperately that she would live to see Christmas.'

'Hannah's youngest brother, Leonard, was about 13 years old at the time. He was a terribly mischievous lad and had been a most unwelcome scholar at all of the various Sunday schools he tried to join, especially as he used to take his pet mice along with him, with which he terrified the girls! However, he had a good voice and he loved singing. It was not surprising then that the enthusiastic, joyful singing at the revival meetings in the new Pentecostal church just down the street from where they lived soon captivated his attention and he became a regular attendee. His mother could not understand why he began asking her for a penny every evening, until he explained where he was going and that he needed the penny to put in the collection box.'

'A.C. Colliss' revival meetings were beginning to gain momentum in Park Street, Alfreton. Very excitedly one night, Leonard rushed home from the meeting and told his parents that the pastor had prayed for sick people that night and that he had seen several people healed. He then announced that the following evening he was going to ask for prayer for his sister.'

'So, the next night he went off to the meeting with great anticipation and as usual during the cold winter evenings, his sister Hannah was carried downstairs and made as comfortable as possible in an easy chair by the fireside. She was unable to do a thing for herself and could never keep a limb still for a moment. She was in a very weak state yet her body looked as though she was in a perpetual wrestling match.'

'Suddenly as she sat by the fire that evening a great calm came over her whole body and she realised that she was sitting perfectly still. Her limbs had stopped flailing and she was at peace. Just then, Leonard came bursting through the back door saying that the pastor had prayed for his sister Hannah and she must surely be healed….!'

'Everyone turned to look at Hannah and they could hardly believe their eyes — she was smiling sweetly up at them as if nothing had ever been the matter with her. The entire family were overcome with joy when they realised that what Leonard had said was true! Hannah was sitting perfectly still; her St. Vitus Dance had gone and she was totally healed in answer to prayer. As for Leonard, he felt as proud as Punch that for once in his life he had done something good!'

'Little Hannah had not walked for the best part of a year, so at first they carried her to the meetings until she regained the strength in her muscles to be able to support her weight. Then she had to learn to walk all over again. She made rapid progress and was soon able to go back to school where, with a little extra coaching from two dedicated Christian teachers called the Wray sisters, she made up for her lost time at school so well that, in her last year, she became the head girl of the school.'

'Dr. Bingham was naturally astounded by the sudden change in Hannah's condition and pronounced it a true miracle. News spread rapidly throughout the town and neighbouring villages of the little girl who had been healed of St. Vitus Dance and Rheumatic Fever. As a result of Hannah's remarkable healing, her mum and dad, Leonard and his brothers Tom, Richard, David and John all became members of the new Alfreton AoG Pentecostal Church.'

'Pastor Colliss preached the necessity of water baptism by total immersion to his new congregation and on 12th January 1929, 17 adults went to the North Wingfield assembly and were baptised there in a large metal tank by the local elder Walter Hawkins (Snr.). These first baptismal candidates from Alfreton included my mother and father and 7 of my relatives. Later, a beautifully tiled baptistery was constructed in the Park Street building and on the 4th May 1929, Hannah's parents, her brothers Leonard, Thomas and Richard as well as Hannah herself were baptised by the elder George Kay. I myself and my 73-year-old grandmother were both baptised on the 6th July 1929. We then all received our baptisms in the Holy Spirit in a series of prayer meetings during the next few weeks. That's how the assembly was founded in Alfreton and both Hannah and myself were there right from the start with our families. We grew up together.'

'Pastor Colliss had hung a number of posters on the wall spaces between the arched windows and both Hannah and myself were arrested by the picture on the panel nearest to the platform on the right-hand side. It was just an outlined map of Africa, white on a black background. It had no geographical features marked on it; no rivers, no lakes, no mountain ranges, no towns or cities, no pictures of animals or any other item to interest a young child – just simply the words: *"Africa waits for Christ."* I felt a strong conviction that the poster was speaking to me and God was calling me to serve Him in Africa as a missionary.'

HANNAH: *'I was healed for a purpose.'*

'When I read the words *"Africa waits for Christ"* on the church poster, I suddenly realised that this was why I had been healed, so that I might serve the Lord in Africa.'

'I will never forget that evening, when Leonard burst through the back door shouting that the pastor had prayed for me at the revival meeting down the road. I knew already that something had happened to me. For a few minutes it had been my little secret. I hadn't dared to tell anyone in case I was imagining things but when they all came to look at me, the evidence was clear for all to see; I had stopped shaking!'

'It was such a relief to be able to reach out for a glass of water and grasp it without knocking the glass over. It was amazing to be able to stand up without my legs buckling under me. I was still very weak but that incessant flapping about of my arms and legs had stopped. I can't describe how grateful I was to God for touching me and healing me. Before that, everyone had been peering at me, expecting me to die at any minute; the house had been quiet like a morgue and no one had dared to raise their voice when I was in the room. But now, the house was filled with laughter again and my voice was the loudest! My mum and dad were kissing and hugging me all over and my brothers were squeezing my arms and legs to check that the shaking had truly stopped. It was like Christmas and birthdays all rolled into one. Praise God! What a miracle — and it happened to me!'

'After that we all started going to the revival meetings. I was a real celebrity everywhere I went. All the neighbours wanted to see me walking and holding out my arms straight without shaking. Our house soon became a drop-in centre for all the young people from the youth group, I suppose because we lived so near to the church. We also used to go to Wesley's house a lot. His dad had many books and was a good Bible teacher so he taught the lads well. Later many of them became pastors and missionaries in their own right. For example, my brother Leonard became the pastor of Bonsall assembly for 21 years and my brother Tom pioneered and pastored a number of churches in Sheffield, including Copper Street assembly.'

'My brothers began very simply by preaching in the local churches as they grew into young men and they were especially welcomed to speak at our parent church in North Wingfield. They often used to testify about my healing wherever they went, so in the end the news spread wider and wider. Eventually, I used to love going to all the yearly conventions at the different churches in the region, where I was often asked to tell my story.'

'Being a farmer himself, our pastor A.C. Colliss was invited by a Christian farmer called William Potter of Chestnuts Farm in uppertown Bonsall, near Matlock to hold a series of special meetings in the Baptist Chapel there. This led to a great spiritual hunger in the village. Walter Hawkins (Snr.) and his wife, Lottie, from North Wingfield later started holding services in Mr. Potter's farmhouse during 1930 and when the front parlour became too small, they moved out into the large barn. I remember that William Potter sanctified the barn by painting *"JESUS SAVES"* in bold letters on the massive barn doors. This attracted a lot of attention in this upland Derbyshire village and these house meetings resulted in the opening of a new daughter assembly, where Mr. Potter became the first pastor in 1934.'

'Strong links were made between the 3 sister churches; North Wingfield, Alfreton and Bonsall, and their young folk formed lasting and sometimes lifelong friendships. It was during this period that I met both Walter Hawkins (Jnr.) who was the organist from North Wingfield assembly and Hilda Potter, the pastor's daughter from

Bonsall. These two later married and became missionaries to the Congo in Africa. I in turn married Wesley Beardsmore and the four of us have been the greatest of friends ever since throughout our years in Africa and to this day.'

'Sadly, my father David Buckley and my brothers Richard and David all died in mining accidents, otherwise our family's tally of preachers could have been even greater. But it all started for our family the day I was healed.'

Alan's Meningitis

Alan Hodson seemed to attract more than his fair share of mishaps as a young lad growing up in the hard days of the Depression. Like many in the mining villages of the East Midlands, his family was feeling the pinch to the point of near starvation at times, which all too often led to chronic illness and deprivation for all but the favoured few in their community.

When he was only 5 years old, he had to trudge to school through a wood alongside his older brothers Leslie and Clifford, his little legs working hard to keep up with them. One day, his oldest brother, Leslie, was giving him a piggy-back on the way home from school to speed his little brother along. It was raining hard and the trail through the woods was becoming a boggy skating rink. They were all cold and hungry and longing for something satisfying to fill their aching stomachs; perhaps their Ma would have made them some bread for their tea?

"Alan, you're getting too heavy for me — I'll have to put you down," Leslie said as he struggled to keep the lively 5-year old on his back. A high bank rose to one side of them so Leslie backed towards it hoping to set Alan down more easily without having to crouch. Unfortunately, Alan's footing slipped and he skidded awkwardly down the bank, landing in a broken heap at the side of the trail. At first no one could touch him, he was squealing so loudly, but eventually his two brothers managed to lift Alan gingerly between them and carry him home to his mother.

The hospital found that Alan had a compound fracture and had broken his thigh in three places, so the leg bones were re-set and he was forced to lie in the hospital bed for 9 long weeks in a heavy cast. At only 5 years of age, he was terribly lonely and frightened. In those days, relatives were only permitted to visit twice a week and Alan's mother, Mrs Pugh, had to climb the stairs all the way to the top of the hospital building to the children's ward to see her little boy. She told him that she could hear him screaming for her when she was in the shop way down in the street below.

Christmas came and went in lonely isolation until the longed-for day arrived when his pot was going to be removed. Alan was a little nervous but pleased at the same time when the nurse came to his bedside with her heavy-duty clippers, but his brave smile soon disappeared as she somehow managed to miss the plaster cast entirely and almost severed his foot instead. Poor Alan was rushed to surgery with blood spurting from his crushed heel and ankle and he had to spend another 4 weeks in hospital recovering from his inflicted wounds! Nowadays, there would have been an inquiry and some talk of compensation - but at that time people were so down-trodden and poor that they learned simply to accept misfortune without question. It was all part of life's rich pattern.

Yet God can use even these difficult passages of our lives to reach us. Alan's accident and subsequent injury became common knowledge in the tight-knit community of Holmewood where his family lived. Not long afterwards when Alan began to fall seriously ill with a life-threatening disease, a neighbour and friend invited Mrs Pugh to the North Wingfield AoG Pentecostal Church and there she found not only Jesus as her Saviour but also a group of people willing to stand by her and pray with her for her precious son. When he was well enough, Alan began attending the Assembly along with his mother and brothers and very soon he accepted Jesus as his Saviour.

He was such a diminutive child from a poverty-stricken family and had suffered so many health problems that my grandparents began inviting Alan to their home. I guess that my Grandma Hawkins wanted to feed the little lad up and also provide a playmate for her only son. This is how my father, Walter, first met Alan Hodson, who was 2½ years younger than him, and their life-long friendship began.

"When I was little," Alan tells me, *"I practically lived at 58 Chapman Lane, Grassmoor with the Hawkins family. I even used to sleep in Walter's bed whenever I got the chance and eventually I spent more time there than in my own home. I loved your grandma and grandad, Pearl. They were very special people and they had a profound influence on my life."*

Dear Alan Hodson recently lost his wife Edith but he is still full of love and gratitude towards his Saviour Jesus and also for all the love shown him by my grandfather Walter Hawkins Senior. *"I can remember him as a gentle giant,"* he told me recently after sharing a meal at our home. *"I don't think I can remember a more humble man in my life."* (It gives you a warm glow to know that your forbears were so well thought of in their generation.) *"There was always encouragement — he always had a kind word for everyone,"* he said. *"Not a great preacher, your grandad, but always a great encourager."*

Then Alan told me his remarkable story of how Jesus healed him:

ALAN: *'I felt a new person. It was unbelievable!'*

'I'd not that long recovered from the episode when I broke my thigh on the way home from school and the protracted stay in hospital that ensued. I was only 6 or 7 years of age and had begun having pains in my chest. Eventually the pain extended down my legs and took me off them altogether. I became so weak I could hardly walk. After I'd been in bed for a week or two my mother fetched the doctor, who concluded that my illness was beyond him to diagnose, so I was carted off to the hospital where the specialist found that I had contracted spinal meningitis. As far as he was concerned that usually led to one of two things; either permanent disability or death.'

'This time I didn't stay in hospital for very long because there was nothing that the doctors could do for me; there was no treatment available and no known cure for the disease. They brought me back home to bed with little hope other than to die. I was allowed no physical exertion and my mother was told that I was not even to tax my brain by talking or reading. I just had to lie in bed, hour after hour, mostly alone and in terrible pain because in those days there were no pain killers available to ease my suffering.'

'I was like that for 2 whole years, scarcely able to leave the bed and only then with strong arms around me to take my weight as I sat on the chamber pot. We had no mod-cons such as indoor toilets in those days and a visit downstairs and across the yard to the privy outside was out of the question. The doctor did nothing for me; he was helpless. My mother could do very little besides feeding and washing me. I felt as if my little life had ended almost before it had begun. Meantime my mother began to attend the North Wingfield Assembly with my two brothers and they were praying for me.'

'After a couple of years my condition began to deteriorate rapidly; I became terribly weak and the pain in my legs was unbearable. I couldn't even lift myself up in the bed. The doctor began visiting regularly and I was in such a state that everyone was expecting the worst. It took a month of intense suffering before mercifully I fell unconscious. My mother was distraught and she ran to the telephone box in the village to send word begging the pastor to pray for me urgently.'

'It happened to be the Wednesday Evening Prayer Meeting that night and as soon as word reached Pastor Wilfred Colliss, he stopped the meeting and told the members that he was going to take the elders immediately to pray with young Alan Hodson who was in a coma. He encouraged the congregation to continue praying meanwhile.'

'Pastor Colliss piled the elders Walter Hawkins (Senior), Clarence Hawksley and Tom Allen into his brand-new car (a rare novelty in those days), and drove straight away to our house in Holmewood. They found me in bed upstairs, unconscious. According to the Scriptures[36], they anointed my head with oil and prayed that God would step in and heal me. That was all that they or anyone else could do. The medical profession had failed me. Bed rest had failed. Now only God could save my life.'

'As they left, there was no sign of any change in my condition; I was pale and motionless — not even an eye flicker. They

---

[36] James 5:14-15a: "Is anyone among you sick? Let him call for the elders of the church, and let them pray over him, anointing him with oil in the name of the Lord. And the prayer of faith will save the sick, and the Lord will raise him up."

clambered down the stairs and having offered words of comfort and encouragement to my weeping mother to keep trusting in Jesus, they took their leave. Now at that time we lived in an old terraced house, so they had to walk down the row to reach the car. My mother waved them off at the door and climbed the stairs to my bedroom. When she entered, she saw that I had my eyes open. With tears filling her eyes she smiled at me and said softly, "*Do you know who's just been to see you?*"'

'"*No*," I murmured. '

'"*Pastor Colliss and the elders from the church; they came to pray for you and they've only just left.*"

'Immediately I got out of bed for the first time in 5 weeks, totally unaided, as if the past 2 years had never happened. I remember I wanted to see the pastor's new car really badly because I'd hardly ever seen a car before, being a poor village lad, so I craned my neck out of the window and began waving furiously. It so surprised the pastor and the elders as they were getting into the car to see me at the window and they waved back excitedly — but they were not half as excited as I was to see that car!'

'The next morning the doctor called by and he had a tremendous shock; I was out of bed and singing the hymn, "*I'll Praise My Maker While I've Breath*"'.

'The doctor said to my mother, "*Who's that?*"'

'"*It's Alan!*" she said, beaming from ear to ear.'

'"*What's happened?*" he asked, confused. "*How can he sing?*"'

'My mother told him about the pastor's visit the previous evening with the elders from the church and how they'd prayed for me.'

'Still astonished and rather dubious, the doctor examined me thoroughly. Finally, he concluded, "*There's definitely something taken place but I don't know what it is. I had come this morning expecting to be signing his death certificate!*" At that he left, still shaking his head in bewilderment. "*I'll call back in a couple of days,*" he told my mother.'

'Soon afterwards Pastor Colliss called by to see how I was getting on. My exuberant singing had grown to a crescendo and everyone began to join in. We had quite a party!'

'When the doctor made his second visit two days later, he had to admit, "*Something's happened. I can't pinpoint it but I see no further need to visit you.*" With that he left. I had been under the doctor throughout my illness but in all that time I had never had any treatment.'

'That Sunday I was at church. There was such a buzz and everyone seemed really glad to see me. Word of my healing had spread like wildfire among the members and all through the locality.

The pastor asked me up to the front to give my testimony of what had happened. I did as best as I could for a 9-year-old but it was hard to explain the whole story because I was unconscious when they came to pray for me. All I knew was that I had been very ill in bed for 2 long years and in a lot of pain. Everyone had been very worried about me and I couldn't remember much after that. Then I woke up suddenly, the pain had gone and I was able to get out of bed and go to the window. It was as simple as that. Mum said that God had healed me when the pastor and the elders came to pray.'

'Pastor Colliss declared, "*It's been a sure miracle!*"' Everyone clapped with joy as I ran back to my seat and we sang our hearts out in that meeting. God was so good to me then and He has been all through my life. I'm in my 80's now but I am still on my feet and still praising God!'

As a sequel to Alan's story, my father happened to be reminiscing about the old days whilst he and I were washing the pots together and Dad told me that he has never witnessed anything quite as moving as when Alan Hodson, aged 9 years, was filled with the Holy Spirit. He was so overwhelmed with love for his Saviour that, kneeling in front of a chair in the vestry at North Wingfield Assembly, he began polishing the seat with his hand in a circular motion and with each stroke quietly sobbing "*Jesus, Jesus, Jesus...*"

"*Of course he loved Jesus,*" Dad said. "*He had been healed and spared an early grave!*"

Joan's Leg

I have fond memories of Joan Topritz (née Taylor) as a bubbly person with a most engaging smile and infectious laugh. When I was a child, she was a loyal member of my grandfather's church in North Wingfield and our families have kept in touch over many years. The story of her healing is a remarkable one. It led to a great revival in the Derbyshire area during the mid-1930s.

WALTER: *'Miracles do happen today!'*

'When I was sixteen years old I witnessed an outstanding miracle of healing in the Assembly of God Church at North Wingfield in Derbyshire. I was the church organist at that time. Our pastor, Wilfred Colliss, had returned from Hampstead Bible College in London full of zeal to take over his late father's pastorate. He had a powerful ministry and often spoke of God's power to do mighty miracles, basing his teaching on the many incidents recorded for us in the Bible.'

'I was the only child of Walter and Lottie Hawkins and we lived in Chapman Lane in the neighbouring village of Grassmoor, which is also where the Taylor family lived. My father was an elder of the North Wingfield Assembly at the time and my mother was a well-known preacher throughout the Midlands area.'

'We had moved into the end house at the bottom of Chapman Lane when I was twelve years of age and I clearly recall that Joan Taylor, then aged eight, was a cripple when we met her. Joan was a pretty rosy-cheeked girl with short, dark hair but she suffered terribly with the crippling effects of a TB hip joint. Her right leg was pitifully thin and shapeless, and it was much shorter than her other leg, making it extremely difficult for her to stand upright. She wore special surgical boots and the knee-length right boot had a platform sole with a five-inch heel built in to enable her to walk. Even with her boots on, though, she struggled to limp along.'

'Joan lived with her parents, her two brothers and one sister halfway down our street. My mother used to make quite a fuss of little Joan, often giving her a big hug as we went past their house. In fact, my parents befriended all of our neighbours and soon gained the reputation of really knowing how to pray for people in need. They were often sent for whenever there was sickness or sorrow in the village.'

'After a while, Joan began to attend our Sunday school with some of her friends. Later, she was in my mother's Bible Class and she also joined our youth group. It used to be distressing to see the poor lass struggling to walk the mile distance to our church, her right shoulder bent over onto her chest for balance as she tried to hobble along on her weak, spindly leg.'

'One Wednesday evening during the summer of 1934, around seventy-five members were present for our weeknight prayer meeting in the Church. That night Pastor Colliss preached about some of the marvellous miracles performed by our Lord Jesus. He reminded us of the Scripture that those who follow Jesus, going into all the world to preach the gospel, would do even greater things than Jesus did.[37] This would confirm their witness wherever they went.'

'Pastor Colliss then invited anyone who wanted prayer to come forward. I was playing the organ softly at the front as about twenty-five people walked down the aisle seeking special prayer for their needs. At the end of the queue, I could see Joan Taylor limping down the aisle to join the others. The power of God was so present with us that I felt something outstanding was about to take place. Pastor Colliss prayed for each one in turn and when the twenty-five had regained their seats, he faced Joan with his two elders, my father Walter Hawkins (Snr.) and Tom Allen, at his side.'

'We all held our breath and cried to God for a miracle as Pastor Colliss began to speak gently to the girl. *"Promise me,"* he said, *"If I pray for you, that you will take this boot off and never wear it again."* I was three yards from Joan at the right-hand side of the platform, still playing the organ but watching her reaction intently. She nodded her agreement and stooped to untie the long laces that secured her black knee-high boot. I saw her fumbling to release the laces from the metal tabs.'

'I will never forget Joan finally unlacing the surgical boot and standing on one foot in front of the pastor, supported by my father on her right side and Tom Allen on her left. She promised to trust God and never use the boot again. All eyes were glued to the thin, dangling foot that was much shorter than the other. My mother was

---

[37] John 14:12 – 'Most assuredly, I say to you, he who believes in Me, the works that I do he will do also; and greater *works* than these he will do, because I go to My Father.'

sitting on the front row and was watching her leg closely from behind. Others were craning their necks to see what would happen.'

'Pastor Colliss anointed Joan with oil and prayed for her in the Name of Jesus. What a miracle! She was healed right in front of our very eyes! Immediately I stopped playing the organ and sat watching, elated and praising God. The folks at the back shot out of their seats and began crowding into the central aisle for a better view. Without assistance and with a big beam on her face, Joan began to walk around barefoot! The place was in uproar with everyone shouting and singing God's praises. The service had ended abruptly but no one wanted to go home. Then the cry went up for someone to fetch a pair of shoes for the girl. There was a family that lived in Lings Row nearby and one of their girls ran home to fetch a pair of normal shoes.'

'There was a spare seat at the end of the front row on the right, so Joan sat down and put on her new shoes. My mother was there helping her with all the other women crowding round. None of her family was with her, since she used to come to church on her own.'

WALTER HAWKINS SENIOR: *'I saw her foot reach the floor.'*

'Pastor Wilfred Colliss was fired up and had simple faith in the Word of God. That Wednesday night, as he usually did when praying for the sick, he called for the elders of the church to stand with him and he anointed Joan Taylor's forehead with oil. He then laid his hands on her head and began to pray.'

'As one of the elders, I was holding Joan's right arm to steady her. I could clearly see that as Wilfred prayed, her foot was still high up off the floor. Tom Allen and I braced ourselves and held her rigidly because she couldn't balance. Then Pastor Colliss commanded her to be healed in the Name of Jesus. Suddenly the power of God came upon her and I saw her foot reach the floor. The whole congregation began to shout and I let her go. She stood amazed for a moment, balancing on both feet, and then she gingerly placed one step in front of the other. Very soon she was jumping up and down with excitement and joy. Praise God! She had been healed.'

'After a while, my wife Lottie and the Hawksley sisters began wondering how Joan was going to get home without shoes. No one had a car in those days and she had a mile or more to walk. Fortunately, someone fetched a pair of shoes that fitted her exactly.'

'Joan left her surgical boot behind that night, so we nailed it up at the front of the church on the partition wall behind the platform for all to see. It hung there for a long time afterwards as a witness to the mighty power of God to heal the sick and lame. News of the healing spread far and wide and later the whole Taylor family became followers of Jesus Christ and joined our church. One of Joan's brothers, Edwin, who was 2 years younger than Joan, later became a leader in the Baptist Church at Paignton in Devonshire.'

JOAN: *'It is and it was a miracle.'*

'Sometimes it brings a few tears when I remember what happened all those years ago. It can be just a simple thing that triggers a memory, such as when I am pouring a bath and the bubbles are rising in the tub. It's like a shiver runs down my spine when I recall that I could never climb into or out of a bath unaided during my childhood years.'

'We were five of us in our family and we were always very poor. We used to live down Chapman Lane in Grassmoor, Derbyshire. Helping my mother in the home was always very hard for me because I had a TB hip and my right leg was five inches shorter than the other. The short leg was horribly thin and frail, while my left leg became strong and sturdy from having to bear most of my weight. I used to be teased mercilessly by the children in our neighbourhood. Mother used to say to me, "*Don't take any notice of them, it'll not do you any good.*" But I used to take great notice of every staring glance and unkind taunt. I was heartbroken at times.'

'Our family doctor was very good. He arranged for me to have a special built-up shoe so that I could hobble around, but I was always left out of the fun and games in the school playground and my dearest wish was to be able to join in the group skipping sessions. Sometimes they would allow me to hold the skipping rope while the others took it in turn to skip in and out, but that was not the same as being able to skip like the rest of them.'

'I started going to Sunday school at the Pentecostal Church in North Wingfield and there I heard Bible stories about how Jesus healed lame people. I desperately wanted to be healed. It was a very long walk to the church and because I had no bus fare, I had to hobble all the way there. My legs hurt, but it was worth the pain just to hear some more about the wonderful things that Jesus did. Later on, I began attending some of the other services too.'

'I was so determined that God should do something for me that I went along to the Church Prayer Meeting one Wednesday evening. When the minister asked if anyone wanted to be prayed for, I went out to the front. The minister said to me, "*Do you realise that the Lord can heal you?*" I nodded hopefully and he began to pray for me. Then he told me to take my surgical boot off. I did as I was told and I had to be held up on each side or I would have toppled over. As the minister prayed again, he laid his hands on my head and asked God to heal me in the Name of Jesus. Suddenly I felt an electric sensation shoot through my body. There was a thud when my right foot hit the floor as my hip twisted back into place.'

'Everyone in the Church gasped when they saw what had happened and I could hardly believe it myself. The minister thanked God for His healing power and he asked me to walk up and down the aisle. I was a little frightened at first because I still limped just a tiny bit and I felt lost without my crutches, but my leg had grown about four inches and everyone began to sing and shout God's praises as I walked unaided. He told me not to put my boot back on but to trust God that my leg would get stronger as I used it.'

'That night I had to walk all the way home in borrowed shoes. Quite a few people walked along with me and Mrs Hawkins came inside the house to help explain to my family what had happened.

My mother couldn't believe her eyes. They could all see the obvious difference in the length of my right leg because I could stand without wobbling over.'

'News travelled fast and it was almost a side show when I turned up at school the next day. Parents had come along just to take a look for themselves at the crippled lass who could now walk. *"Hey, you're not Joan Taylor!"* one said to me in disbelief. I had no crutches and most of the kids thought it was great. *"March up and down,"* they ordered gleefully. Some of the children made fun of me, though, as I still had a slight limp.'

'After my healing, my mother started to attend the North Wingfield Pentecostal Church with me. It made quite a difference to her attitude towards my problems. When I used to come home in tears because of all the gossip at school, she would say, *"Let's pray about it."*'

'My grandfather didn't want to believe that I had been healed to start with. He told me, *"When they took your boot off it didn't go down well with me."* Yet even he had to admit in the end that it was a miracle that I could now walk unaided.'

'Of course, the time came to visit our family doctor. He had known me all of my life. I can't remember whether he measured my leg before and afterwards. I'm not even bothered about that. The fact is that it is and it was a miracle and I do remember the doctor telling me, *"You have been healed."*'

'At fourteen years of age, the most important change for me was that at last I could skip like all the other children. We used to tie the rope to a lamp post and all the other children used to gather round to watch me skipping for all I was worth. It was a wonderful feeling, to be accepted at last.'

'A few years later I overheard an old school friend talking about me. She said to her companion in her broad Derbyshire accent, *"Oh, that were Joan Taylor. She went to school with me. She had a bad leg, then all of a sudden she hadn't got one!"* I had to chuckle to myself.'

'There was another very important outcome of my healing. The doctor had told my mother that I would never be able to have children because of my TB hip. But God thought otherwise. In due course, I married and gave birth to three healthy boys. I am now eighty-three years of age[38] as I recount my testimony to Pearl and I thank God every day that He healed me.'

Doreen's Lumps

Our family have enjoyed a very close relationship with Doreen Rushton ever since she started attending the Station Road Assembly in Carlton, Nottingham in 1977. Doreen is a nurse and she has the most caring and loving personality. I remember how she would visit my mother at home when she was very poorly and Doreen would cut

---

[38] Joan Topritz lived to the ripe old age of 86 years, sharing her golden wedding anniversary with her husband Gerald and other family members on Christmas Eve 2007 during the last week of her life. In all the years since her remarkable healing, she loved and served God faithfully.

up a slice of buttered toast into tiny pieces so that Mum would not have to struggle to cut it herself with her arthritic fingers.

This is Doreen's remarkable testimony of how God healed her shortly after she became a Christian.

DOREEN: *'Thank you God.'*

'My mother died in 1976 and naturally I was totally devastated. When Pastor Len Patchett of the Station Road Assembly took the funeral service, I sensed God's love reaching out to me and this was a huge comfort. I felt God calling me to turn back to Him and for almost an entire year God continued to talk to me and comfort me. This to me was quite miraculous that I, Doreen Rushton, should be communicating with the God of the Universe. Eventually on the 8th of May 1977, I asked God to forgive me of all my sins and I committed the whole of my life to Him. Immediately I felt like I had come out of a dark tunnel: the sky was bluer; the grass seemed greener; birds were singing with such joy. Suddenly an immense peace filled my whole being and I couldn't stop praising the Lord. This salvation experience completely changed my life.'

'Shortly afterwards a lump started to grow on the front of my neck. Over the next few years the increasing size of the growth caused me a great deal of trouble. I was scarcely living - merely existing. My weight went down dramatically to 7 stone 4oz and I began to be breathless climbing stairs. At times I lost my voice completely and could not speak. At best I could only talk with a husky voice, often in a whisper.'

'Then another lump began to grow on the side of my neck and my doctor suspected that it had originated from the first lump. This led to further problems with my throat that frightened me. Sometimes food would get stuck when I tried to swallow and I would choke. My condition began to be increasingly painful and invasive until finally I was taken down to the hospital theatre to have the first lump taken out. Imagine my disappointment when I regained consciousness to find that they had only removed the smaller lump from the side of my neck. The surgeon explained to me that they had decided during the surgery to leave the first lump alone because of where it was situated unless it became a matter of extreme urgency to remove it.'

'In 1982 I was again admitted into hospital for emergency surgery due to the severe narrowing of my throat but the lump at the front of my neck still remained.'

'There were times when I felt very low. At such times I found that the Lord was a safety net underneath me and when I read my Bible, the story of Job really helped me. We had a new pastor by then at our church, Pastor Hawkins. Looking back, I feel very grateful and privileged to have known such caring people as Pastor Len Patchett, Pastor Walter Hawkins and his wife Hilda Hawkins.'

'One day I asked Pastor Hawkins for help and he came to visit me. He was a great support and he prayed with me and encouraged me to trust God. Over the years I had often asked the pastor and the elders of the church to pray for me and each time it was like receiving a good dose of medicine. But I was still suffering.'

'Then one Sunday, the Holy Spirit urged me to go forward for prayer again during the evening service. Pastor Hawkins was preaching. As he prayed for me I saw the heavens open and I heard wonderful music. I felt the most wonderful anointing come over me and I sang in the Spirit for the very first time with words I did not understand. Then a prophecy was given over me that I would be healed but that I would have to travel a long, hard road.'

'When I arrived home, I was worse than I had ever been before but I rebuked the pain as I knew in my heart that God had touched me. From that night the growth began to shrink until just a tiny pea-sized lump was left to remind me of where it had been. Even though the hospital was reluctant to discharge me at the time, the lump never grew back again.'

'I am so thankful and praise the Lord for my healing. I just want to shout, "*Glory to God!*" When I look back, I wish that I had testified more about the healing at the time. Now, if I could put my healing into a bottle and give it out, I would.'

Marian's Breast Lump

Marian Rashleigh's family claim to fame is that her great uncle Ralph escaped from the sinking Titanic and survived. In her own right, though, Marian has been a devoted supporter of missions for many years, particularly in South America. At home, she cares for her disabled brother Ken but still finds time to make pots of jam to raise funds for the missionaries and orphaned children of Brazil. She puts a picture of a child on each pot of jam that she sells — *'They're going like hot cakes!'* she tells us happily in her regular news bulletin.

At one Missionary Conference that my father was convening, Marian had a developed a lump in her breast and she was very anxious about it. Desperate to be healed, she came to my parents for prayer:

WALTER: *'Marian is a grand girl. I don't know another one that can touch her.'*

'When Marian Rashleigh knocked on our chalet door at the Missions Conference, Hilda and I were surprised to see her looking so drawn. I assumed that the fact that she had been responsible for setting up the Conference Exhibition had been taking its toll on her.'

'Hilda and I invited her in for a cup of tea and then she explained about the lump in her breast. It had been getting progressively bigger and was causing her a great deal of concern. She was obviously worried that it might be cancer. Immediately we prayed with Marian very definitely about it. Within a short while the lump had disappeared and it has not been a problem since!'

'Marian is now very active around the world in Missions and her work has been recognised by the AoG churches who have granted her a Worker's Certificate. I don't know any other lady anywhere who has stood so faithfully on her own all across South America in places like Brazil, and in many European and East

European countries, to support missionaries and reach people with the gospel.'

'On top of this, she is a good platform speaker and she always used to organise the AoG Conference exhibitions everywhere. She is a tireless worker for Jesus Christ.'

Andy's Colitis

Andy himself has been a miracle to our lives.

We first met Andy Griffiths in 2003 when our family moved to Barlborough and we started to attend Hope City Church in Sheffield, South Yorkshire. We must have brushed shoulders a few times in church and later as carers for the south region we would sometimes gather at Andy and Sarah's house for progress meetings. We got to know the whole family even better a couple of years later when we were all invited to a house-warming barbeque by some mutual Hungarian friends Csaba and Eva.

In 2008, our business at The Sofa Studio in Chesterfield, Derbyshire was forced to close due to the onset of the Credit Crunch and world recession. My husband, Mick, had earned very little for many months prior to that but he was determined not to sign up for unemployment benefit, preferring instead to trust in God's provision.

Meantime our pastor David Gilpin advised Mick not to look for only one option at a time but to try at least 10 different avenues of enquiry simultaneously in order to find work. Armed with this valuable advice, Mick began knocking on every door that he could think of and 'phoning all his friends and acquaintances for openings. By the time we reached option number 38 we gave up counting!

Poor Mick … First, he tried setting up an internet site for re-upholstering furniture but at the end of 12 months, his costly and beautiful web-site had not generated a single enquiry. Meantime he set up a business buying and selling cars with my cousin, David, just as car sales slumped to an all-time low. After that debacle, Mick and David wondered about buying and renovating dilapidated houses and they were just about to make their first investment when the housing market collapsed. So that was another non-starter.

In desperation, Mick began valeting cars for neighbours, giving personalised sales training to friends at church and even offering guitar lessons — anything to earn a few pounds here and there.

That summer, a Christian friend told Mick that he felt God had given him a prophetic word that Mick should not accept the first job that he was offered. A short time later, Mick was indeed offered a direct sales position selling mobility equipment to disabled people. Since he had been recommended to this position by a former colleague who knew what a good salesman he was, Mick did not like to decline the offer. He was very hopeful during the training period, but after a few days on the road he realised that the company's sales methods were non-ethical and after 8 weeks he left. Thank God that he did: shortly afterwards the directors of the firm were arrested for dishonest sales practices. Mick knew then that he should have listened to God instead of clutching at straws, no matter how dire our financial situation might be.

All this time, we were living on very little income and caring for my parents in our home, so that the only reliable income we had was my weekly Carer's Allowance, then £49. Since our food bill alone amounted to over £130, it takes little deduction that our reserves were diminishing fast with all the household bills to pay. Week by week, we kept trusting in God and praying for His answer to our need for work and a reliable income. My mother, Hilda, was housebound and becoming increasingly disabled and weak so that I could not sensibly look for work or leave my parents for any length of time, day or night. The onus was on Mick alone.

As winter 2008 approached, Mick began applying for any and every job that he could possibly tackle, but even so there were very few jobs to apply for in the papers and Job Agencies were a complete waste of time. He even began applying for temporary Christmas positions and part time posts — anything to earn some money. He still refused to sign on at the job centre for a hand-out because he truly felt that God is our Provider ('Jehovah-Jireh') and that He would use what is in our own hands and the skills that we have. All we needed was God's direction for our lives, so we prayed and continued to pray for a breakthrough.

One Wednesday evening in late October, we attended a Partner's Meeting at Hope City Church. We *just happened* to sit next to Andy Griffiths who asked how things were going. Mick told him about a job he had been offered that day as a part-time shop assistant in a local Spar shop. We felt bad about the job because it would mean that Mick would have to miss Sunday meetings.

'You can't do that!' Andy exploded. *'It's ridiculous, a man of your talent. It's such a waste!'*

After absorbing what Mick had told him for a minute or two, Andy suddenly turned to Mick and enquired, *'Are you handy at all?'*

Mick didn't have to think very hard to give an answer; his father Graham was a builder and hobby mechanic so Mick had grown up being 'handy' every time his Dad did a job around the house or on the car! It was always, *'Mick, hold this,'* or *'Mick, fetch that,'* and *'Pass me that spanner over there,'* or *'Mix some more cement!'* Later on, Mick joined his father in the building trade for a couple of years before he went into sales.

So, the answer was a simple *'Yes'*.

Andy beamed. *'Would you like to come and work with me?'* he asked.

Mick was flabbergasted. We had prayed together that afternoon for God to lead us in our decision-making and here was the answer — *'No'* to Spar and *'Yes'* to Andy's kind offer. Mick knew that Andy's mate had been ill for several weeks with pneumonia, so although the offer was initially to fill in for Jonathan (another of our Hope City friends), Mick knew instinctively in his spirit that this was God's provision, no matter how temporary it might be.

So began another chapter in us learning to trust God day by day and week by week. Andy was very pleased with Mick's efforts as a jobbing mate fitting kitchens and bathrooms. Meantime Jonathan told Andy that the work was too physical for him, especially after being weakened by pneumonia and his wife's business as a letting agent was taking off so well that he had decided to help her instead. This left the position open for Mick to fill, which he did with gusto.

The only problem for us was that Andy only needed Mick a few days here and there, as the need arose and contracts allowed, so our financial provision was a drip-feed. However, we are eternally grateful for Andy's intervention and for God's sustaining power through the difficult 'Credit Crunch' and ensuing world recession.

ANDY: *'I didn't expect a miracle.'*

'When I was young I frequently suffered with severe abdominal pain culminating in acute diarrhoea and bleeding. After various tests the consultant diagnosed me as having ulcerative colitis, a serious intestinal disorder that, if it persists, can eventually lead to colon cancer. My symptoms were almost continuous so I was given corticosteroid drugs and my mother was told to feed me a special diet and give me vitamin supplements to reinforce my body's defences.'

'I was told by the consultant that I was also suffering from anaemia caused by frequent blood loss. He warned me that complications such as rashes, mouth ulcers, arthritis and conjunctivitis are common side-effects of the disease. Periodically I had to visit the hospital for further blood tests, colonoscopies and biopsies to check for the development of cancer, so I was quite worried about the whole thing. Several years went by and despite the drugs and treatment, I wasn't cured. Chronic bouts of diarrhoea and bleeding accompanied by fever and abdominal pain kept recurring, far too often for my liking!'

'When I was 17 years old, I went to a meeting at a local Vineyard Church and during the service people were invited out for prayer if they needed healing. At the time my symptoms were really bad and I was in terrible pain so I went forward, but I can't say I really expected much to happen. I guess I just hoped something might. I can't remember much about that evening, except that someone gently prayed with me that God would heal me of my colitis. The pain left me and I've not had a bout of colitis since! I just want to thank God because I'm able to eat normally; I have a lovely wife and 2 gorgeous children, and my life has been transformed.'

Willie Burton's Abdominal Cancer

I cannot close this chapter without mentioning the miraculous healing of pioneer missionary and field director William F.P. Burton, who is mentioned several times in this book. He was a modern-day apostle and I had the great privilege of knowing him personally and giving up my bed for him to sleep on whenever he came to stay at our home; he used to love my mother's cooking!

I have many special memories of him: from sitting on his knee as a child, spellbound whilst he performed one of his many conjuring tricks for me ... or watching him write 'JESUS SAVES' on the beach at Marsden Rock (when it was still there) near Sunderland ... or listening to him expound his doctrine about the timing of the Second Coming of our Lord Jesus at our home in Carlton, Nottingham (a topic that my mother was hugely interested in) ... or watching him painting one of his many masterpieces, both here in England and in the Congo – he even painted a sketch of the beach at Marsden in my Autograph Book for me, under which he wrote, *"Jesus, Thou who tamed the rolling seas, guide my erring footsteps and bring me safely home at last."* I say "Amen" to that!

Willie Burton lived so near to God that when he was struck down with abdominal cancer in 1944 aged 58 years and was given 6 months to live, he was quite happy to go or to stay. He was ready to *'be with Christ, which is far better'*; however, he felt that, if it was God's will, it would be more helpful to the Congo Church *'to live on in the flesh'*, as he had left certain work unfinished. Like the Apostle Paul, he was *'hard-pressed between the two'* but wanted, like Paul, that Christ should be *'magnified in my body, whether by life or by death'*.[39]

---

[39] Phil. 1:20-23

My parents had just arrived on the CEM mission field that year; this was a horrifying blow to them, as novice missionaries, for they had been aspiring to follow in Mr. Burton's footsteps and learn as much as they could from such a giant of the faith about soul-winning and church planting.

Willie Burton had been used by God to bring healing to a multitude of people, by the laying on of hands and prayer. For example, in 1908 aged 22, even before he had set out for the Congo, Willie was working as an electrical engineer when one morning he was called upon to pray for a girl aged 18, a member of his church choir, who was so sick that she was not expected to live until midday. His manager reluctantly gave his permission for Willie to rush to her bedside.

The doctor in attendance said that the girl had been coughing up blood along with bits of her lungs, and that she could die at any moment. Willie Burton placed his hands on her in the Name of Jesus and prayed, then hurried back to work. The girl stopped coughing at once and was soon up and about. Later she married, and 57 years later in 1965, she wrote to Willie Burton as follows:

'Dear Mr. Burton, you asked me to have an X-ray. I have had one and am sending it to you, trusting it will be to the glory of God. I was 18 when the Lord healed me and I shall be 75 this month ... He is the same yesterday and today and forever ... I never forget to pray for you ... Yours in Him, Alice Eccles (Rossall).'

The Certificate was from Manchester Regional Hospital Board and said:

'Thank you for your co-operation. You will be pleased to learn that your chest X-ray was satisfactory on 27th April 1965.'

Willie Burton had always been keen to have miraculous healings verified and certified after the event, to the Glory of God. And now he was facing sickness and a death sentence himself.

A basic caecostomy operation was performed on Mr. Burton in Johannesburg, South Africa, leaving him with a faecal bag inserted to evacuate his intestines. However, a year after his return to Mwanza to die, and after much prayer on his behalf, Willie Burton's natural functions were restored and in 1946, the hole in his side was closed up by surgical operation in Luanshya, Zambia. The doctors could not believe that this was the same man who had presented, according to his X-rays, with terminal cancer 2 years previously!

My father Walter Hawkins was at the railway station to greet Willie Burton on his return after having X-rays to verify this miraculous healing.

"Ne muntu mutuntulu!" he cried in Kiluba to my father as he leaped from the high carriage step of the steam train, his face beaming from ear to ear. *"I am a whole man!"* he shouted.

After that, Willie Burton returned to normal life, being more active in his later years than most men of his age. The whole story, with X-ray photographs, is told in his book *Signs Following*. He eventually died in January 1971 aged nearly 85 years, having lived a full and productive life of ministry right up until the end.

CHAPTER 6: Divine Providence

'Trust the past to the mercy of God; the present to His love; the future to His providence.' ST. AUGUSTINE

The Pioneer Missionary's Larder

In 1944 during the Second World War, my parents Walter and Hilda Hawkins travelled via convoy, dodging German U-boats and mines, down the coast of Africa and up the Congo River into the interior, where they served as missionaries in the Congo Evangelistic Mission for 16 years. They were only 27 and 26 years old when they arrived, penniless, in the Congo; they had spent all their resources during the tortuous 10-week journey and had given their last coin to the lad who helped them with their luggage. Thankfully some kind missionaries were waiting to greet them and give them shelter until they could forge on towards Kabondo Dianda, their first mission station. My parents learned the Kiluba language by simple gesticulation without any dictionaries or language aids and armed only with two essential words that enabled them to communicate.

"I kika?" – *"What is it?"* they would ask the curious children that were happy to hang around these strange 'white spirits' who had set up camp in a tent near to their village. My father would write

down phonetically each word along with its meaning until he had built up his own mini vocabulary. He was quick to learn. Only 16 weeks later he preached to the nearby community and despite his faltering delivery, two villagers accepted Jesus as their Lord and Saviour – the first of many tens of thousands that he won for Christ in the Congo.

During the following year, my father founded 13 churches in the area at the rate of one a month, all built with the help of the locals, and *"Running, well running!"* as he put it, with the most enthusiastic converts in charge. My father would teach these potential leaders, most of whom were totally illiterate and they would then pass on what they had heard to their local communities, and so the good news of the gospel spread like wildfire in the region.

It may have seemed quite a daunting challenge for my young parents to pioneer churches in largely unreached regions of central Africa where the inhabitants had been held for centuries under the evil domination of witchdoctors and despotic chieftains. However, their efforts and those of dozens of other fledgling missionaries had only been made possible by the selfless and daring exploits of the mission founders William F.P. Burton, whom I called Uncle Burton, and his co-founder James Salter, who first entered the Congo in 1915.

'Jimmy' Salter was the son-in-law of the great British healing evangelist Smith Wigglesworth and he was a close family friend of ours. In fact, only a year before my parents arrived in Kabondo

Dianda, my parents had asked Jimmy Salter to marry them in Bonsall, Derbyshire in January 1943.

Willie Burton with Alice (Smith Wigglesworth's daughter) and
Jimmy Salter

Uncle Willie Burton was an amazing missionary preacher and he would typically share the following account to illustrate how wonderfully God provided for him during the ensuing years when he was pioneering the vast Congo interior of 910,000 square miles, half of which was dense forest and where many earlier missionary pioneers had perished due to insect-borne plagues such as malaria and black water fever. Willie Burton liked to be considered just a 'tramp preacher' because as he would often explain, it was said of Jesus Christ that '*He went about doing good*'[40], which meant quite simply that Jesus tramped from village to village preaching, teaching, helping people and healing their diseases. And so Willie Burton wanted to be nothing more than his Lord, a humble tramp preacher. In fact, *"Not I, but Christ"* was his life's motto.

WILLIE BURTON: *'I would gladly go into any fever-stricken hole in the Name of Jesus, because "Greater is He that is in [me] than he that is in the world.[41]"– There are millions of dark heathen who don't know Christ and I must live to carry the Gospel to them.'*

'I was walking and cycling, where possible, from our base in Mwanza to a very distant mission outpost in Kipushya, some 15 days' journey away. It meant tramping through swamps, crossing rivers, following narrow jungle tracks or battling through dense undergrowth with machetes, whilst contending with unbearable heat, electric thunder storms and the unwelcome attention of harmful creatures. Each night my carriers and I would face the ritual of setting up camp in any clearing we could find and at first light we would pack up our belongings again, not knowing what each day would bring.'

'There was urgent Mission business to attend to and time was of the essence so we pressed forward, paying little attention to the myriad flies that swarmed to lick our sweat, or to the blood-sucking ticks that clung like limpets to our flesh. Each evening clouds of malaria-bearing mosquitoes would rise from the swamps in lethal assault on

---

[40] Acts 10:38
[41] 1 John 4:4

any living creature they could find. Thus, I succumbed and fell sick with a high fever, too ill to walk or cycle, so had to be carried in a hammock. This greatly impeded our progress so that our food supplies quickly ran out.'

'"*Lord,*" I prayed, "*Please provide meat for my hungry men as I have no strength left to hunt.*"'

'Just then, the men carrying my hammock stopped in hushed silence. One of them whispered in my ear, "*I can see an antelope over there.*" He pointed toward the tall elephant grass ahead of us where I could just make out two horns. The antelope would have been staring directly at us, having heard our group advancing from some distance. I expected at any moment that it would bolt and that we would not see it again.'

'"*Do you think you could shoot from the hammock?*" the carrier asked anxiously. He could see the sweat pouring down my face but he knew that I had a gun by my side (it was necessary to be prepared for all eventualities in the tropical forests).'

'I cautiously lifted myself onto one elbow, picked up my ready-loaded rifle and aimed carefully between the two horns that were visible above the grass. The antelope moved its head. Was I too late? Would it leap away at any moment? My hands were shaking and my vision blurred from the fever. I aimed again just a little lower this time and fired.'

'The horns vanished momentarily ... only to appear again. My porters groaned with disappointment since they considered me to be a dead shot. *"My hands must be shaking too much,"* I thought as I sank wearily back into the hammock. I would not normally miss at such a distance. I wiped the sweat from my brow with my sleeve, then propped myself up again and took aim. The antelope was motionless, surprisingly unperturbed by the gunshot. The men braced themselves to hold the hammock rock-steady this time as I fired my second cartridge. The shot rang out and the horns vanished ... only to appear a third time!'

'"*It must be this fever,*" I muttered, wiping the sweat from my eyelids with the back of my thumb. All were acutely aware of our pressing need for sustenance and the men's stomachs had been rumbling in anticipation. *"Lord, help me!"* I thought, *"We need this animal."*'

'The antelope remained rooted to the spot, transfixed, its horns just visible as before. It was staring directly at us and I could sense the motion of its tail flicking nervously in the elephant grass. I mustered all my remaining strength, prepared my rifle with trembling fingers, then steadied my aim and fired.' Again, the antelope horns disappeared and blades of elephant grass parted.

'Exhausted, I clung to my rifle, my whole body trembling from the concentrated effort. The men stood motionless for a few moments, hardly daring to breathe. But the horns did not reappear this time and as the baggage carriers leapt forward, I sank back gratefully into the hammock.'

'Elephant grass was flying in every direction. All of a sudden, the porters let out a shriek of delight, for they found not only one dead antelope, but three in a row! Every shot had found its mark after all! With no regard for my fevered condition, my hammock bearers dropped me unceremoniously on the ground and rushed to join the celebration as they all danced around the kill, howling like a pack of hyenas.'

'"*God heard the bwana's prayer,*" someone shouted. They all looked back at me and then one by one they dropped on their knees crying, "*God is real! God is good! He has answered prayer!*" Jehovah-Jireh - our Divine Provider - had more than abundantly supplied our needs. What a campfire meeting we had that evening! Much strengthened, we were able to complete our journey and continue the work of God in Lubaland.

Hannah's Tick Fever

My parent's close friends, Wesley and Hannah Beardsmore, were married during the Second World War in 1942. Hannah, you may remember, had been healed from St. Vitus Dance and Rheumatic Fever as a 10-year old child in Alfreton, Derbyshire. In 1949, the couple were sent out as AoG missionaries to open a new field in Tanganyika Territory (now called Tanzania). Then in 1951 they were asked to transfer to Baraka in the former Belgian Congo and in 1952 they opened a new mission station at Lulimba in the Fizi Territory of Kivu Province, Congo.

The Beardsmores were blessed with 3 children - Heather, Ralph and Graham - who all attended the same boarding school for missionary's children as I did. The school was run by a lovely group of American Brethren teachers at Sakeji near Kitwe in the former province of Northern Rhodesia (now Zambia). I used to sit next to Graham Beardsmore in class and I remember being in total awe of his sister Heather Beardsmore who was several years my senior and had the most gorgeous long plaited hair down to her hips. How I longed to be elegant and beautiful like her!

Hannah Beardsmore's medical work was brought to an end by the Simba rebellion of 1964 when their family was included in a group of 10 adult missionaries and 4 children held captive by the rebels for 129 terrifying days. Their life's ministry was shattered and sadly the hospital and school buildings that Wesley had erected were all destroyed.

WESLEY: *'Without God's intervention, Hannah would have died.'*

'The first indication of God's providential concern for our future wellbeing came about during the Christmas break prior to our captivity by the Simba rebels in 1964. We had to make a long journey of over 1,000 miles southwards to the Copperbelt town of Kitwe in Zambia to pick up our sons, Ralph and Graham, from the mission children's hostel where they and other children were cared for by former CEM missionaries, Horace and Elsie Butler.'

'By the time we got there, Hannah was feeling very ill and feverish so I put her straight to bed not realising how seriously ill she had become.'

'It so happened that Hannah and I had been hoping to contact the Zambian Red Cross in the hope of obtaining urgent medical supplies for our hospital back at Lulimba. Horace and Elsie told me that Dr. Hannah, the chairman of the Red Cross, happened to live nearby but that he was a very busy man and often travelled to far flung places as part of his duties.'

'That evening I took a stroll down the street to enjoy the cool evening air and clear my thoughts. I was getting worried about Hannah's condition; she was running a very high temperature and obviously had picked up a nasty infection of some kind. Just then I happened to come across a gentleman in his front garden. We started chatting and I was pleasantly surprised to find that it was Dr. Hannah himself. When I told him how ill my wife was after our long journey he kindly offered to come back with me to see her. The verdict was not very good: he confirmed that she had a form of malaria and he promised to return the following day to see her. Meantime we had to keep her as cool as possible and give her plenty of water to drink.'

'The next morning the doctor found Hannah to be much worse and he suspected that in addition to malaria, she also had contracted smallpox and possibly tick fever. I was panic stricken. Any one of these dreaded conditions could rob Hannah of her life, so what chance did she stand with all three? Dr. Hannah pulled a very powerful magnifying glass out of his doctor's bag and started to examine every inch of my wife's body. Eventually he found the head of a bush tick that had embedded itself in her skin. Immediately he was able to prescribe life-saving treatment.'

'Since Dr. Hannah was the Chief Medical Officer of Health for the copper mines, he was able to arrange for a nurse to come each morning and evening to attend to Hannah and administer the potent drugs that would save her life. Hannah was isolated in a side bedroom all over the Christmas period. Dr. Hannah himself called in as often as he could on his way home from work and we had very interesting conversations as he told us of his early childhood in Derbyshire and I described our missionary work in the Congo. His father had been the rector of the model village of Endsor on the Duke of Devonshire's Chatsworth Estate, so Dr. Hannah had spent many years in the lovely park that I myself had visited many times as a youth with my best pal, Walter Hawkins, on our regular cycling rides around the Derbyshire hills and dales.'

'Was this chance meeting with an eminent doctor, one who hailed from our own part of Derbyshire, within hours of our arrival in Zambia at the very time when Hannah needed urgent medical attention — was it just a mere coincidence? I don't think so. Without immediate medical intervention or a miracle, Hannah most probably would have died. God was in control!'

'After Christmas, Dr. Hannah promised to take our request for medicines to the next board meeting of the Red Cross. When at last Hannah was feeling better, he dismissed our anxious questioning about how much his bill might come to and how we should be able to pay for the essential medical supplies for our hospital. He said there would be no charge at all. The Red Cross committee voted to give us a donation of £100 (quite a substantial sum in 1964) to buy medicines from Holdsworth's, the largest chemist supplier in the Copperbelt. The MD asked us to make out a list of our requirements and promised to charge everything at cost price, thus greatly increasing the amount we could buy. The list of medicines that Hannah ordered included many that could only be obtained with a doctor's prescription.'

'Then we had the problem of transporting all those heavy boxes of medicines across 1,000 miles of bumpy roads and dirt tracks to our remote mission hospital at Lulimba. With God's help we were able to buy a good second-hand trailer that served us well and when we eventually arrived home, we had the largest and best stock of medicines in the whole of South Kivu Province! Again, I affirm that this was no mere coincidence. God knew what lay ahead for us in the future months with the onset of the Simba uprising and He was making vital provision for our safety and for our medical needs.'

The Building of North Wingfield Church

When we Christians dare to undertake a major project under the inspiration and guidance of God's Holy Spirit, we can almost surely expect resistance from our enemy, the devil[42], because he doesn't like to see God's Kingdom advancing, nor God's children being blessed. The devil's forte is discouragement; his trump card, delay.

In the early days of the Pentecostal revival in Britain, many tiny house groups were soon bulging at the seams as new members joined the fellowships meeting in front parlours all around the country. Very soon it became a matter of urgency to acquire or build permanent churches so that the congregations could grow. Many opted for upper rooms in public buildings, or shared premises with other organisations, but other groups were more enterprising, wanting a purpose-built church of their own to worship in.

One such congregation in North Wingfield, Derbyshire was led by a very energetic and capable preacher called Arthur C. Colliss. The year was 1925. My grandparents were just becoming interested in joining the new charismatic group and in fact they were present at the opening of the new church building. Little did they realise at that time the terrible trial that AC Collis had endured to

---

[42] 1 Peter 5:8 "Be sober, be vigilant; because your adversary the devil walks about like a prowling lion, seeking whom he may devour."

bring the embryo church into existence. This endeavour had nearly cost him his life:

WALTER: *'God had covered it already.'*

'It's not cheap or easy work building churches! Arthur C. Colliss found that to his cost. He had managed to secure a plot of land beyond the end rows of terraced houses called Lings Row that marked the boundary between Grassmoor and North Wingfield. The plot was adjacent to the crossings on the old colliery railway line so I guess that it must have been relatively cheap as no one would want to build a house right next to a busy railway line.'

'It just so happened that AC Colliss used to deliver milk to our house in those days, being a local dairy farmer. He knew that my mother was a preacher on the Methodist circuit and so they often had discussions about the Bible, especially relating to the promise that Jesus made before He left this earth that He would send the Helper[43], God's Holy Spirit, to be with His disciples, to lead them into all truth.[44] My mother was intrigued by his words and started looking up the Scriptures herself and praying about them. Eventually she agreed to come to the new church when it opened; she would bring me and my father with her.'

---

[43] John 16:7 "Nevertheless I tell you the truth. It is to your advantage that I go away; for if I do not go away, the Helper will not come to you; but if I depart, I will send Him to you."

[44] John 14:26 "But the Helper, the Holy Spirit, whom the Father will send in My Name, He will teach you all things, and bring to remembrance all things that I said to you."

'All was proceeding well with the building of the church until AC ran out of money. The situation was desperate; the poor members had contributed all that they could afford and more besides, considering that they were suffering great hardship and deprivation during the Depression years. But despite every fund-raising effort their bank manager was threatening to foreclose on the building loan and AC Colliss stood to lose everything he owned including the farm, which was his livelihood.'

'AC was totally at the end of his tether; he had tried everything. His health was suffering from all the stress and he had completely run out of ideas. The deadline for paying the bank had arrived and he had nothing left to give. There seemed to be no other option but to abandon North Wingfield church and say goodbye to all their efforts.'

'That afternoon, AC was up in the mill next to the farmhouse. He was so devastated by it all that he had hung a rope over the rafters and was pacing up and down, building up the nerve to hang himself. It seemed the only way out; he couldn't bear the shame of failure and losing everything he had worked so hard to achieve. He couldn't face his family, nor could he face his congregation who had all sacrificed so much to pay for the building. All afternoon he had been weeping and praying, beseeching God to step in and provide the money to meet the bank instalment, but the heavens had seemed like brass. Where was God when he needed Him most?'

'Little did he know that 60 miles away in Birmingham, God had already been speaking to a chap called Harold Rowe, a godly man whom AC had met at a recent Stephen Jeffreys campaign[45]. The Lord told Harold to take a certain sum of money, which was a huge amount in those days, and take it immediately to Mill Farm in Derbyshire and give it to Arthur Collis.'

'"*Where is he?*" Harold called when he finally arrived at the farm.'

'"*Over at the mill*," he was told.'

'He could hear the babbling stream and the wheel creaking as he turned away from the farm door so he strode towards the sound.'

'"*Arthur!*" he called as he approached the mill house.'

'Inside, AC had been adjusting the noose, lost in his troubled thoughts; all hope lost, his faith abandoned.'

'"*There you are!*" said a startled Harold, dumbstruck to see this beloved Christian pastor with a noose above his head.'

'AC fell to the ground sobbing, his broad shoulders heaving in time with his cries.'

'"*What are you doing, man?*" asked Harold, shocked to see Arthur in such a terrible state. He didn't like to think what might have happened if he had arrived a moment later. He recalled suddenly how God had told him to hurry, to leave straight away, but

---

[45] See Chapter 1: "The Jeffreys Phenomenon."

there was so much to do first before he could set off on his journey. By the looks of it he had only just arrived in time!'

'AC looked up at him with a tearstained face. He couldn't speak. Through his tears it was hard for him to recognise this man whom he had only met briefly once or twice before. *What did he want?*'

'"*God told me to bring you some money. Here, look, here it is!*" Harold reached in his jacket pocket and drew out a thick wad of notes.'

'The tears started to flood down Arthur Colliss' face. God hadn't abandoned him after all! How foolish his lack of faith seemed to him now as the shuddering emotions in his breast subsided. With a little encouragement from Harold, he got to his feet and began to count the money, one precious note at a time.'

'"*It's exactly what we need! The exact amount!*" Arthur roared, not knowing whether to laugh or to cry.'

'After that episode, AC Colliss was transformed into a man of tremendous faith. God had tested him to the utmost limit and yet his faith had not only survived the ordeal but was all the stronger for the testing. Finally, AC did it; the building was opened on December 26th 1925. Ours was one of the first purpose-built churches of the Assemblies of God and I was there at the opening ceremony, a lad of only 7 years, squeezed on a bench between my Mam and Dad. We joined the church and AC Colliss' ministry affected all our lives in a powerful way after that. I have lived to be truly grateful for the enormous sacrifices made by this great servant of God.'

North Wingfield Assembly of God, at the time of its opening.

Ruth's Hot Water Bottle

Our close friends, Mac and Margaret Fox, delighted us recently by sending us this account of a wonderful miracle provision, written by an American doctor working in Central Africa.

DOCTOR: *'Before they call I will answer.'*[46]

'One night I had worked hard to help a mother in the labour ward; but in spite of all we could do, she died, leaving us with a tiny, premature baby and a crying 2-year old daughter. We knew we

---

[46] Isaiah 65:24

would have difficulty keeping the baby alive as we had no incubator – in fact we had no electricity to run an incubator – nor did we have any special feeding facilities.'

'Although we lived on the Equator, nights were often chilly with treacherous draughts, so one student midwife hurried to fetch the box we kept for premature babies along with the cotton wool that the baby would be wrapped in. Another student went to stoke up the fire and fill a hot water bottle.'

'The latter came back shortly in distress to tell me that in filling the bottle, it had burst! Unfortunately, rubber perishes easily in tropical climates.'

"*And it is our last hot water bottle!*" she exclaimed.'

'In the West we would say, "*It's no use crying over spilled milk!*" Similarly, in Central Africa it might be considered no good crying over burst hot water bottles; they do not grow on trees and there are no drugstores down forest pathways! We just had to get on with things and do what we could.'

"'*All right,*" I said, thinking on my feet. "*Put the baby as near the fire as you safely can, then sleep between the baby and the door to keep it free from draughts. Your job is to keep the baby warm!*"'

'The following noon, as I did most days, I went to have prayers with any of the orphanage children who chose to gather with me. I gave the youngster various suggestions of things to pray about and told them of the tiny baby. I explained our problem about keeping the baby warm enough, mentioning the burst hot water bottle, and that the baby could so easily die if it got chills. I also told them of the 2-year old sister crying because her mother had died.'

'During prayer time one 10-year old girl, Ruth, prayed with the usual blunt conciseness of our African children. *"Please God,"* she prayed, *"Send us a hot water bottle today. It'll be no good tomorrow, God, as the baby will be dead — so please send it this afternoon!"*

'While I gasped inwardly at the audacity of the prayer, Ruth added, *"And while You are about it, would You please send a dolly for the little girl so she'll know You really love her?"*'

'As often with children's prayers, I was put on the spot. Could I honestly say, *"Amen"*? I just did not believe that God would do this. Oh yes, I know that He can do everything; the Bible says so — but there are limits, aren't there? The only way that God could answer this particular prayer would be by sending me a parcel from the homeland. I had been in Africa for almost 4 years at that time, and I had never, ever, received a parcel from home yet!'

'"*Anyway,*" I thought, "*If anyone did send me a parcel, who would put in a hot water bottle? I lived on the Equator!*"'

'Halfway through the afternoon, whilst I was teaching in the nurses' training school, a message was sent that there was a car at my front door. By the time I reached home, the car had gone, but there on the front porch was a large 22-pound parcel. I felt tears pricking my eyes. I could not open the parcel alone - this was a big event to celebrate - so I sent for the orphanage children who gathered around me excitedly, full of expectation. Together we pulled off the string, carefully undoing each knot so we could save the string for some other purpose (you learn to be thrifty in Africa!). We folded the paper, taking care not to tear it unduly. Excitement was mounting. Some 30 or 40 pairs of eyes were focussed on the large cardboard box.'

'From the top, I lifted out brightly-coloured, knitted jerseys. Eyes sparkled as I gave them out. Then came some knitted bandages for the leprosy patients — the children looked a little bored and disappointed — but after that I pulled out a box of mixed raisins and sultanas. That brought a cheer because it would make a nice batch of buns for the weekend!'

'Then, as I put my hand in again, I felt the… "*Could it really be?*"… I grasped the neck and pulled it out. "*Yes!*" A brand-new rubber hot water bottle emerged. I cried. I had not asked God to send it; in fact, I had not truly believed that He could.'

'Ruth was in the front row of the children. She rushed forward, crying out, "*If God has sent the bottle, He **must have** sent the dolly, too!*"'

'Rummaging down to the bottom of the box, her little fingers probing expectantly, she pulled out a small beautifully-dressed doll. Her eyes shone! She, Ruth, had never doubted! Looking up at me, she asked, "*Can I go over with you and give this dolly to that little girl, so she'll know that Jesus really loves her?*"'

'"*Of course,*" I replied!'

'That parcel had been on the way for 5 whole months, packed up by my former Sunday School class, whose leader had heard and obeyed God's prompting to send a hot water bottle, even to the Equator! Also, one of the girls had packed in a special dolly for an African child — 5 months before — in answer to the believing prayer of a 10-year old to bring them, "*This afternoon.*"'

'Prayer is one of the best free gifts we receive. It doesn't cost us anything, but it reaps a lot of rewards. When you read this, say a prayer for whomever you want. That's all you have to do. This awesome prayer takes less than a minute. No strings attached...'

'"*Heavenly Father, I ask you to bless my friends reading this. I ask you to minister to their spirit. Where there is pain, give them your peace and mercy. Where there is self-doubting, release a renewed confidence to work through them. Where there is tiredness or exhaustion, I ask You to give them understanding, guidance and strength. Where there is fear, reveal Your love and release to them Your courage. Bless their finances, give them greater vision, and raise up leaders and friends to support and encourage them. Give each of them discernment to recognise the evil forces around them and reveal to them the power they have in You to defeat them. I ask You to do these things in Jesus' Name. Amen.'"*

CHAPTER 7: Angelic Visitation

'... some have unwittingly entertained angels.'[47] THE APOSTLE PAUL

Much has been written over the centuries about angels. Each of us have our own mental picture of how an angel should appear and often this is derived from the traditional concept of a shining being with wings and perhaps even a halo, dressed in an iridescent white gown. Yet even in the Bible, there are many varied descriptions of angels, some with and some without wings and each type bearing their own specific title such as 'cherub' or 'seraph'. *The Bible Reader's Encyclopaedia and Concordance[48]* defines angels as: *'Messengers of God whose task is to do God's service in heaven, or to aid and succour men on earth.'*

In current writings and from the experiences I have heard about, it would appear that an angelic being can take on many different forms and sizes. So how is it possible to distinguish an angelic visitation from simply a coincidental event? Perhaps only in the eye of the observer, who feels that the being they have witnessed is a supernatural entity, can true revelation be found.

---

[47] Hebrews 13:2
[48] Collins Clear-Type Press; First Edition (1962)

In his book entitled, *"...and then I saw Him"*[49] Rev. Samuel Doctorian says, 'As I witness about those angels I have seen, I want to make *sure* to say that they were not impressions, they were not dreams, they were not even visions or just my own imagination. They were real, heavenly beings just like you read in the Holy Scriptures, in the Old and New Testament. Angels created by God, ministering spirits who have faces. They have glorified wonderful bodies, who speak, who can see, who have ears to hear. They are in the unseen world where physical eyes cannot see them. There are thousands upon thousands of those heavenly beings. I do believe, as the Word of the Lord says also, that He has His angels, guardian angels[50] with every child of God; an angel that the Lord has given to minister to us, to protect us, to bless us and to guide us. And if God sees it necessary for us to see those angels, He would touch our eyes and open our eyes so we can see those heavenly beings.'

It is possible that these angels play a greater role in our day to day lives than any of us care to imagine. If we think back very carefully over our lives we may well recall events when, for example, we could have been injured or even died, but something special happened just at the right moment to avert the danger. There may also be times when a material provision has landed right out of the blue just when we needed it most.

---

[49] Bible Land Mission (1990)
[50] Matthew 18:10 – "Take heed that you do not despise one of these little ones, for I say to you that in heaven their angels always see the face of My Father who is in heaven."

Not everything in life can be put down to mere coincidence. So, enjoy the following accounts taken from the experiences of people we, or our friends, know personally. Multiply these visitations across each family on earth and you may get an idea of the prolific nature of such events.

Mum's Hunter

HILDA: *'My life was saved by an unusual looking angel.'*

'My midwifery work in the Congo left me with very few opportunities to join my husband, Walter, on his frequent missionary trips into the villages scattered across our region and along the banks of the Congo River. On one occasion, however, he arranged that I should meet him halfway through his itinerary at a certain village so that we could spend a little time together. I was to travel on my bike with a sixteen-year-old lad to guide me through the forest and the plan was that I would be able to meet the villagers and share the meeting around the bonfire with Walter before returning the next day.'

'The journey started out well enough. The lad and I took a lift as far as possible on the mission vehicle and then we set out through uninhabited bush land in the direction of the village. I tried not to think about the wild animals that might be lurking about in the undergrowth but kept my mind solely on peddling carefully through the tall grass and undergrowth that was pressing in on either side and trying to avoid any rocks or ruts along the way. The lad ran along ahead of me and it was all I could do to keep up with him under the circumstances.'

'All was well until the narrow path started to descend sharply and the noise of pounding water began to fill me with dread. I hesitated on the damp path lined with dead leaves and piles of debris that had been washed down by the recent rains. It was safer to dismount but then my feet sank into the soggy mulch. Somewhat amused, the lad took charge of my bicycle for the steep descent and I squelched along behind him, grabbing whatever I could for support. Then as we rounded a bend in the path I stopped dead in my tracks. A huge river, swollen and roaring through the cutting, was pounding the rocks below. It was an awesome sight. The span was so wide that two gigantic trees had been felled, one on either side, which met in the middle of the river with their heavy branches entwined to form a makeshift bridge to walk over. This would have been a fearful contraption for me to balance upon at the best of times, but after heavy rainfall, the river was bursting its banks and sweeping all before it. One slip and I would have drowned in the torrent. I had never learned to swim properly since an accident as a child in a swimming pool had made me very fearful of deep water. I was rigid with fear since from experience I knew that I always slipped even on the smallest branches straddling the tiniest brooks. I looked at my young and very diminutive companion and I could see that he would never be able to save me if I fell. Even if I crawled along, with the river surging around me and its turbulent waves lapping over the wet tree trunks, I knew that I could not cross over safely.'

'As I stood surveying the scene in dismay, I suddenly felt searing pin pricks all over my ankles and rising rapidly up my legs. "*Quick mandamo, move away!*" the lad shouted in Kiluba, his native tongue. "*You're standing in a line of paji ants!*" I looked down with renewed horror. These marching ants can strip a human body in no time at all if left unchecked! The stinging of their bites increased in intensity with every second that I hesitated. With a squeal, I jumped away and the boy helped me to pluck off the myriad of ants that by now were crawling all over my clothing and biting the exposed flesh on my arms and legs.'

'After we were done, the lad picked up my bicycle on his shoulders to cross the river. I suppose that he was used to taking such risks and he was certainly very sure-footed with his bare feet. He almost ran across the tree trunks as I looked on in astonishment. But then I froze as abject fear overtook me. I simply could not follow him.'

It was at that moment that God's deliverance came. Every detail is still vivid in my mind even after all these years. A pair of legs seemed to alight on the path behind me and touch the ground gently, almost in slow motion. Then from around the bend the form of a hunter came into full view. What a sight he was! A native, naked except for a loin cloth around his girdle and long strings of beads and other artefacts hanging from his neck. In his hand was a spear. It must have been four feet long. He came to where I stood and I looked at him fearfully. My heart was pounding more than ever. Inside I was wondering, *"What next?"* I was fearful for my life.'

'He spoke to me in Kiluba. *"What is the matter?"* How did he know I was in trouble? Perhaps he could see it on my face. I replied in the native tongue, *"I am afraid to cross the river."*'

'*"Come here,"* he said. *"Take hold of this."* He thrust the shaft end of his spear into my hand and before I could remonstrate, I found myself being pulled onto the first tree trunk. I have never known anything happen so quickly or so perfectly as what happened next. He passed over the trees with the speed of a deer and I followed just as quickly, clinging for all I was worth to the spear. As I sped across, I could feel some of the paji ants nipping my scalp. They had reached the hairline under my sun helmet and were biting me for all they were worth.'

'I guess the ants were the least of my worries. I was practically bounding along the tree trunks in my slippery shoes and the spear was forging ahead of me like an arrow in slow motion. I scarcely had time to notice the spray from the waves drenching my feet. Before I knew it, we were over and I remember thanking the hunter profusely. Then he disappeared up the path in the direction of the village. Meantime, I dashed into the tall grass at the side of the river for privacy as I tried to pluck the remaining paji ants from under my clothing and out of my hair. Talk about ants in your pants! It was not a pleasant experience at all.'

'Once I had recovered sufficiently to continue our journey, I clambered up the bank and climbed onto my bike again. My young companion had witnessed the whole saga and was waiting patiently for me to join him. We continued up the path and once the roaring of the river had subsided we began to hear faint singing in the distance. Gradually the singing grew louder until we caught sight of a group of Christians singing for all they were worth and clapping as they approached. They had been watching out for us and had come to welcome me to their village. In the centre of the crowd was my husband, surrounded by several ululating women who were cupping their hands over their mouths and howling for all they were worth. It was such a welcome sight, after all those days of separation.'

'My first question to Walter after we had exchanged hugs and greetings was, "*Did you see a hunter coming up this path a moment ago?*" "*No*," he replied. We asked the members of the crowd who had been looking out for me to arrive. Their answer was a unanimous "*No*." I was mystified. How could they not have seen him? Once the band of trees lining the river was passed, the area opened out towards the village and they were bound to have spotted anyone walking in that direction, even if he had left the path. Nor did any of them recognise my description of the man. It was as if he were from another world, another place, another time.'

'Since all that happened to me, I have heard many instances of angels appearing in different forms and then vanishing. I am sure that God sent an angel to help me cross the river safely that day. The length and strength of his spear had been the perfect instrument to help me to balance along the slippery tree trunks despite the turbulent water rocking such a makeshift bridge. He was the only person I had encountered on the whole journey.'

'God sent the perfect answer at the exact time that I needed it. It was awesome.'

Marlie's Father

On 7th July 2007, Mick and I attended my cousin David's wedding at a Baptist Church near Potter's Bar, London on a very rare sunny afternoon during the otherwise wet summer of that year. It was the first time that I had met his beautiful Egyptian bride Basma and she looked stunning in her cream gown with lace top as she came down the aisle on the pastor's arm, preceded by my niece, Claire, and her 4-year-old son, William, who was happily scattering rose petals from his basket. Mick and I were really looking forward to spending a wonderful day out with them — we were not to be disappointed.

Mick was an usher and David had asked me to read 1 Corinthians 13 – the 'Love Chapter', as it is sometimes called. I had chosen the 'Living Bible' version but before it was my turn to read, Basma's sister went to the lectern to read the same Scripture in Arabic. Knowing the verses so well, it was fascinating trying to match up the strange words she was pronouncing with the words in English. When I sat down after my rendition, Basma beamed at me with the most welcoming smile and I knew that we would be good friends. You somehow know these things when you meet someone, as if you'd been friends forever.

The reception was held at a magnificent hall in Epping Forest, whose lawns dipped down to green meadows and a wide vista of luscious farmland on the distant hillside. David had kindly arranged for Mick and me to sit with a group of Basma's friends from the Baptist Church and the family we sat next to had provided the music for the wedding service. The pianist Marlies, who originated from Germany, told me this remarkable account of when her father met an angel:

MARLIES: *'My father still talks about it with awe.'*

'I was brought up in a little village called Wölmersen south of Cologne in Germany during the austere years following World War II and the defeat of the Nazi regime.'

'Like all the other young men of his time, my father, Erich, had been drafted as a young recruit into the German army and he was one of those poor unfortunates who had to fight in appalling and often freezing conditions on the Northern Front, with very little protective clothing and inadequate ammunition. He was only 17 years old when he was captured during the epic fighting between the German and Russian armies and he ended up in a Russian prisoner of war camp.'

'The German POWs were treated harshly by their captors and were set to work with very little food or shelter from the bitter cold.

Many did not survive the rigorous conditions. There were rumours of live experimentation going on using the POWs as guinea pigs and quite a number of prisoners would systematically disappear. None of the prisoners knew what to expect next; the uncertainty, cold, fear and deprivation made even the strongest grow weak and despondent.'

'It was only his faith in Jesus that kept my father going under these circumstances and after a while he managed to find 4 other young Christian prisoners in the camp. The group of 5 met regularly whenever they could to pray together and share their experiences. They used to repeat the few Bible verses they knew from memory and encouraged each other to trust that God would protect and help them during their terrible suffering.'

'One day, while they were huddled together in a little room praying, they each became conscious that there was an additional 6th person in the room kneeling next to them, not just the 5 friends who had entered at the beginning. Each took the opportunity to take a peek at the new prayer partner; none of them had ever seen this person before and none of them had been aware of anyone entering the room. The group continued praying in turn as normal, each privately curious about whom this person could be. With this new addition the prayer meeting seemed far more thrilling and meaningful than ever before but as soon as they had finished praying, when they all sat up and opened their eyes, they were amazed to find that the person had gone.'

'The 5 young Christians were so encouraged as they each confirmed and discussed what they had seen. None of them had heard the door open or close, neither before nor after the person's visit. Surely, it was decided, they would have been very aware of any footsteps in the vicinity in case a guard should find them huddled together praying, because gatherings of any kind were strictly forbidden in the camp. They each confirmed that they had never heard any movement of any kind; all they knew without any doubt was that one minute the person was there with them and the next, he had disappeared. Each was aware that the visitor had stayed during the whole time that they were praying. They also agreed that in such an enclosed community of prisoners, they had all been surprised to see a total stranger in their midst. Surely they would have known his face and at the very least would be bound to see him again somewhere in the camp. After extensive enquiries, they realised that no one in the camp knew who he was and they never again saw the person.'

'Finally, the friends concluded that there was no other explanation but that they had been visited by an angel. This encounter was such a great stimulus to the young lads. They realised that God had not forgotten their plight; He had heard their prayers and had sent His angel to be with them to encourage and support them. It was just what they needed to see them through the bitter days of their captivity.'

'My father is over 80 years old now and he still talks about his experience with great awe.'

The Angelic Teacher

WALTER: *'During 1950 -51 John Emmett and I were in neighbouring Mission Stations.'*

'During the 1930s and 40s, the north of our Katanga region was slowly being opened up by missionaries Fred and Isobel Ramsbottom from their mission station at Katompe. After we returned to the Congo from our first furlough in 1950 with our newborn baby, Pearl, my wife, Hilda, and I were asked to continue the work in Kongolo that had been started by Elvin and Phyllis Lee. Some 30 miles south of Kongolo on the road to Katompe, new missionaries John and Ruth Emmett had been opening up a brand-new mission station during 1949 at Katea and very soon they became our lifelong friends. Every time they needed supplies, they would travel to the shops in Kongolo where we were stationed and then call at our mission house for tea and fellowship on their way home.'

'John and Ruth stayed at Katea for 2 terms between 1949 until Independence in 1960 when we were all evacuated from the Congo by the US Forces. During that time John Emmett, who was a great evangelist, frequently made forays into the surrounding villages to preach the gospel and plant new churches. It is in one of those villages that this remarkable miracle occurred:'

TSHOMBA: *'I never went to school.'*

'I was brought up in Northern Katanga in a village near Katea, the main Congo Evangelistic Mission station for our area. My father was a farmer with a small patch of land cleared from the bush. We lived entirely on what we could grow ourselves or barter with other villagers - things like manioc, sweet corn, mangoes, bananas, peanuts and palm nuts for oil. My mother kept a few scrawny chickens for eggs and meat. It was a simple life and we had no schooling, so I never learned to read or write. It didn't bother me because I saw no need for education; my only aspiration was to clear my own garden patch and become a farmer like my father, which I did.'

'My family accepted Jesus Christ as our Lord and Saviour when Bwana John Emmett visited our village and I became a faithful member of the church that the new converts built. The missionary sent a young pastor to look after our church but some years later he was invited to pioneer a church elsewhere which meant that they would need someone else to look after our church in his place. It was a big responsibility for any man and we were all very sad to see our beloved pastor leave.'

'To my surprise the main pastor in charge of the Katea church asked me to visit him at the mission station. After a few pleasantries he astonished me by saying,'

'"*Brother Tshomba Léon, you are a trustworthy and faithful fellow and I want **you** to take the services at your church, at least for the time being until we can find a suitable replacement. It will be your job to beat the tam-tam drums to call the villagers to church* *and I want you to preach the Word faithfully and teach the people about Jesus. I will come and visit you after a while to see how things are going. Meantime, I am relying on you, Tshomba, to fill the gap for me.*"'

"'*But I...I can't read*," I stuttered, turning a pale shade of grey. I was amazed that the station pastor would even consider someone like me. "*I never learned to read*," I repeated deliberately to make sure that he understood my predicament, "*And I don't have a Bible, so how can I teach the people?*"'

"'*God will help you, Tshomba. I'm afraid there is no one else I can ask, so you will have to do what you can and rely on God for what you cannot do.*"'

'That was it. I was in over my head. I returned to my village in turmoil; what was I going to tell everyone — that I had been promoted to being their new leader?'

'The first service I had to take was the Wednesday afternoon Prayer Meeting. That wasn't too difficult because of course we had lots to pray about and once I got the meeting started everyone else took over the praying. It had been a shock losing their precious pastor and now this upstart was leading the meetings! No wonder they prayed so fervently!'

'However, I was dreading the Sunday meetings. My heart pounded and sweat poured from my palms at the mere thought. I had no idea how to prepare a sermon, let alone how to choose a subject to preach on. It all seemed hopeless to me. Then the station pastor's words, "*Do what **you** can and rely on God for what you **cannot** do,*" kept ringing in my ears.'

'I decided that the only thing **I** could do was to fast and pray. Thursday, Friday and Saturday passed. I did not eat a morsel and only drank a little water to keep myself alive in the heat. All the time I shut myself away in my hut and cried out to God for His help. I needed a word from Him to give to the people.'

'Then during the night on Saturday, a man dressed in brilliant white robes came to me in a vision. He was carrying a book and he placed it in my hand.'

'"*Tshomba Léon,*" he commanded. "*Take the book and read it!*"'

'Shaking with fear and awe, I looked at the book. I had never owned a book; I had hardly ever held one before and my fingers were fumbling with the pages to open it. It never occurred to me to remonstrate that I could not read. I had to do as I was bidden; there was no other choice.'

'Somehow I knew that it was the book of Daniel. Then as I opened the pages I found that the words made sense. It all became clear to me in an instant.'

'"*Read!*" commanded the shining being.'

'I began to read the words from the page in front of me. I realised immediately that God was preparing me to preach His Word.'

> "*Blessed be the name of God forever and ever,*
> *For wisdom and might are His.*

And He changes the times and the seasons;

He removes kings and raises up kings;

He gives wisdom to the wise

And knowledge to those who have understanding.

He reveals deep and secret things;

He knows what is in the darkness,

And light dwells with Him.

I thank You and praise You,

O God of my fathers;

You have given me wisdom and might,

And have now made known to me what we asked of You...".[51]

'Then the vision left me.'

'Early on Sunday morning before the cock had crowed I rose quickly and dressed. My heart was pounding in my chest. The vision had been very clear and the image of the shining being was still very vivid in my mind. But I had to know for sure that I could really read. This was something too amazing for me to contemplate.'

'I knew that one of the Christians in the village possessed a Bible so I ran to his hut and banged on his door to wake him up.'

'"*What do you want at this time in the morning. It's not light yet!*" he grumbled.'

'"*I've come for your Bible. Quick, I need it!*"'

'After a little shuffling and mumbling, my friend cautiously opened his door. He could not understand why I could possibly want his Bible because he knew for a fact that I was not able to read.'

---

[51] Daniel 2:20-23

'"*I have a sermon to prepare and I need your Bible,*" I insisted. Reluctantly he brought me his prized possession. Not many owned the Word of God in those days, not even many of the pastors.'

'I grabbed the precious book from his hand and opened it.'

'"*Look and listen!*" I ordered, my voice quivering in eager anticipation. To my great relief and his even greater surprise, I began to read clearly as if I had been reading all my life.'

'My friend's jaw dropped. "*What in God's name — what has happened to you?*' he exploded.'

'"*Hallelujah!*" I shouted excitedly and continued to read at the top of my voice, rousing the neighbours from their sleep. I didn't care — the more I read, the more I wanted to read. I babbled on until he could stand the suspense no longer.'

'"*How come you can read, my friend?*" he kept asking. "*Tell me what has happened!*" Finally, he shouted in my ear, shaking me by the shoulders, "*Tshomba, my dear brother, this is a miracle! Explain to me how you can read.*"'

'Finally, I calmed down enough to tell him about the vision and how I had been given the book of Daniel to read by the shining being.'

'"*I now know how Daniel or Isaiah must have felt, when the angel of the Lord appeared to them,*" I chuckled, thrilled to be reliving stories from the Bible in my own lifetime.'

'Suddenly we couldn't help ourselves; my friend and I began jumping up and down for joy, shouting and praising God at the top of our voices.'

'By now the neighbours were bursting from their huts to see what all the commotion was about and very soon the news that a remarkable miracle had happened was spreading like wildfire throughout the village. Everyone woke early that morning. The women of the village were ululating excitedly and everyone was talking at once. There hardly seemed any point in sounding the drums for the start of church. It seemed like the whole village was there to witness their new pastor preach his first sermon and read from the Bible.'

'I preached about the Good Shepherd and when I made an appeal, several villagers raised their hands and accepted Jesus as their Saviour. I was delighted. God was confirming to me that He wanted me to pastor this church. Best of all, He had already equipped me to preach His Word by giving me the astonishing gift of being able to read.'

The Mystery Plumber

I had just moved to a new city with my two young daughters when we found ourselves gripped in the throes of a severe cold spell. I had very little money in the bank and was still awaiting my first monthly pay cheque from my new job. The house was freezing cold and when we awoke the next morning, we found that the central heating had stopped working and there was no running water. We couldn't even make a hot cup of tea to warm ourselves.

Dreading the potential cost, I searched through the Yellow Pages for a plumber without any success. It appeared that there were burst pipes and worse throughout the entire region and every plumber everywhere was in great demand. I was becoming desperate because I knew no one in the vicinity and we had nobody to help us. I began to pray. After a vast number of telephone calls, I eventually found a plumber from a one-line advert in a local free paper who was willing to come and have a look.

The man arrived almost immediately to inspect the situation. He scrambled up into the loft where he found that the pipes leading from the header tank had little or no insulation, which was why the water in them had frozen solid. For more than an hour he heated the pipes with his blow torch in an attempt to defrost them, but without much success. I remember him clambering down his ladder in a filthy state from all the dust in the loft, with a dejected look on his face. The task was taking far too long and he had a list of other calls to make. Hurriedly he left instructions to leave the trap door open with an electric heater blowing in the room below. He said he would return later on to take another look. I was grateful for his help but dreading the mounting costs.

True to his word, he did return later that day at about 6pm. This time, he spent an hour and a half heating the pipes carefully with his blow torch. He was very cautious in case the frozen pipework would burst. Downstairs, I was waiting anxiously and praying. At last the good news came: he had achieved a breakthrough. It took him another half hour to insulate all the exposed pipes for me and then he prepared to leave. With my heart in my mouth, I asked him how much I owed him. He said he wasn't sure and that he would send me a bill.

That was the last I heard from him. After a week had passed, I tried to find his name and telephone number in the next free paper that arrived, but it was nowhere to be found. He must have only advertised in the previous week's paper and unfortunately that had been thrown in the bin. I never did receive a bill despite all the hard work the man had put in, plus the cost of the gas he had used in his blow torch and all the insulation materials. Including a standard call-out fee, I had estimated that the bill was likely to have exceeded £100, which I could not have paid at that time.

I have often wondered since what really happened. Whenever I read the Scripture that tells us that sometimes we entertain angels unawares, my mind immediately thinks of my generous helper in that freezing cold November weather. Who knows? Angel or not, I'm sure that he was God's answer to my predicament that day.

CHAPTER 8: Demonic Powers

'... I give you the authority to trample on serpents and scorpions, and over all the power of the enemy...'[52]

LORD JESUS CHRIST

The Kinkotonkoto Driver

When my mother and father arrived at Kongolo in the 1940s, they were appalled to find themselves occupying a shack that looked rather like a triple garage without doors. It comprised three open-ended compartments in a row without windows or interconnecting doors. The end 'room' was totally unusable as it was entirely filled with an anthill that had swallowed up the earth floor and had long since risen up into the roof. The other two 'rooms' had ceilings that were ballooning down with the weight of the anthill that had spread throughout the roof space. The whole place looked as if it could collapse in a deadly heap of wriggling termites at any moment — the weight would most certainly kill you. In fact, it was probable that the only thing keeping the structure even remotely stable was the rigidity of the sun-baked skeleton of the anthill that had grown steadily like a creeping paralysis throughout the whole building.

---

[52] Luke 10:19

Worse still, there was not even a door to protect my parents from wild animals at night or from the stares of the inquisitive natives by day. All Dad could do the first evening was to pile up their packing boxes across the door opening and rig up their camp beds for the night. Needless to say, they didn't sleep very well.

During those first few weeks, the packing boxes were all they had for furniture — table, chairs, writing desk, storage cupboard. Just keeping the streams of ants away from their meagre provisions and swatting the pesky flies seemed a full-time job. Even Dad's precious reference books and his Bible were being chewed at remorselessly. What the ants missed by day was soon polished off by their night-time rodent visitors. You might be forgiven for considering the elephant-nosed mice with their long, twitchy snouts quite cute in comparison with the elephantine rats that scurried up and over the boxes and into every crevice searching for left-over morsels from the day before.

Only the hastily rigged mosquito nets kept my parents relatively safe from the marauding rodents and inevitable snakes that preyed on them. As darkness fell, they could hear a host of menacing noises — strange snufflings and scratchings outside. Far too close for comfort, hyenas barked and cackled mockingly whilst leopards stalked in the undergrowth beyond the sandy perimeter of their compound. Only the occasional beam from Dad's flash-light reflected in pairs of eyes from near and far would reveal the whereabouts of individual predators. The makeshift toilet happened to be a hole in the ground well away from the shack - not much relief there for the terrified pair!

Such was my parent's arrival in Kongolo.

A secure door to their sleeping room was a first priority the next morning and Dad soon managed to nail some scraps of wood together so that they could sleep in relative safety. Then began their main task as missionaries ….

My father soon realised that the only way he would be able to share the love of God with the local people was the same way that Jesus himself adopted when He started His early ministry: it would take a miracle. First there was the language barrier and then there were the local superstitions and natural prejudices to overcome.

Dad soon set about walking around the locality, trying first a smile, then a wave to any passers-by. One day he came across a lady who appeared to be in great distress; her husband had undergone a dramatic and sudden change and consequently, was no longer able to work as a lorry driver. Dad set out to visit the afflicted man …

WALTER: *'It would take a miracle.'*

'A crowd had gathered around the hut but I went in to see the man alone. When I entered the hut, the man was lying curled up in a ball on the floor; his hair was matted and he stank from stale urine and saliva. He had been frothing at the mouth. It was very apparent to me from the outset that the man had been possessed by a demon.

The abrupt change in his character and his total incapacity to speak anything but profanities was a clear indicator.'

'I asked him if he wanted to be free. I explained how Jesus, the Son of God, had come to earth; how He had died to set us free from the powers of darkness and from sin. I told him that the result of sin is certain death, but that Jesus came to forgive us of our sins and to bring us new life.'

'I told the man that he would have to truly want to be set free.'

'He nodded in agreement, unable to utter a word.'

'I commanded the man to stand up. I prayed for him to be set free from the demonic power in the Name of Jesus that is above all other names.'

'Suddenly the man fell flat on his back. He did not crumple or try to protect himself from the fall but was completely pole-axed, lying rigidly on the floor. Then he opened his eyes and smiled at me for the first time.'

"God has set you free!" I said. My heart was dancing.'

'The next day when I visited Kinkotonkoto village, I found that the man was out driving his lorry. The whole village was buzzing with the news of his transformation and of course his wife was delighted because he would be able to provide for them once more and wouldn't be beating up on her as before.'

'That Sunday, the lorry driver was in church and he publicly accepted Jesus Christ as his Saviour. Alongside him sat his wife and relatives. In fact, the entire family accepted Jesus and that was the beginning of the remarkable work that God did for us during our time in Kongolo.'

NB: A local evangelist (Alube) was sent to help Dad during those early months at Kongolo Mission Station. When Alube saw what God had done for the lorry driver, he was fired up! He followed Dad everywhere and many miracles followed as the two of them prayed in the Name of Jesus for the sick in the surrounding region. Many new churches were opened!

Teddy Hodgson's Riverboat Revival

Edmund Hodgson was a very special treasure to a little missionary kid like me. I simply adored him.

Growing up in the Congo, I had virtually no children's books to read and few toys to keep me occupied. My main enjoyment was to play hopscotch in the sand using an old mango seed, or to climb trees under the watchful eye of my African nanny, who herself was only about 11 or 12 years old (after which she would be married off). Sometimes we would make holes in the anthills that riddled the mud brickwork of our house, then poke a grass stem into the exposed channel to retrieve any guardian ants that clamped onto the stem with their pincer-like mandibles. My nanny would quickly detach them and squash their large orange heads between her thumb and middle finger before throwing them into her mouth and swallowing them whole without a care - to her they were like a tasty sweetie! Personally, I never could quite pick up the courage to try one and I'm glad now that I never did because most of the local Africans' stomachs and intestines were pitted and scarred where the sharp pincers, some of them still nipping, had pierced their insides!

So the days passed by, interrupted only by violent electric storms and the odd brush with a snake, giant spider or chameleon. But a visit from 'Uncle Teddy' as I called him would brighten up my sheltered existence: he would open up worlds to me that I knew nothing of. For example, he could mimic all sorts of animal noises and would fascinate me with African folklore tales!

TEDDY: *'We were on the eve of another revival along the Congo river.'*

'In 1950 I finished the latest Bible Schools for my village evangelists with special meetings for receiving the Holy Spirit, and each evangelist went home on fire. Very soon I could see the results. In many churches every soul, both men and women, laid prostrate before God and were not able to get up until they were right through into the Pentecostal experience of speaking with tongues.'

'Some received the baptism in the Holy Spirit whilst still in the river after being baptised. Others awakened in the middle of the night, as they received the baptism in the Holy Spirit in their huts. Some hardly knew what the blessing was that they had received and were so happy they couldn't keep quiet in the church services. Thus, I had to type out a special sheet of Scripture references to help them, whilst I was on the riverboat, in which I briefly stated: *(1) What speaking with tongues is; (2) What it is for; (3) What it is not for; (4) What gifts are to follow if they go on.*'

'In one village a whole secret society of wicked men and women, fifty in all, who had been terrorising the villagers for many years, were converted after the church members prayed and fasted for them for 33 days.'

'In another village an old chief had a vision of God's glory that lasted for 14 hours! As in a trance, he came into the daybreak service with hands outstretched to God in worship. Everyone in the church fell down under the weight of the glory of God and many were baptised in the Holy Ghost. When the old chief finally 'came to earth' at four in the afternoon, he immediately called for the village evangelist, confessed his sin, accepted Christ as his Saviour and then told of his vision of Hell and then of Heaven. Shortly afterwards, I baptised him in the river.'

'A demon-possessed woman was delivered from the demonic power that had controlled her for years after her entire local church prayed and fasted for 3 days for her deliverance.'

'The evangelists delayed me in every village to ask advice, as the spirit of expectancy was so high and their folk didn't want to leave the meetings. I have been amazed by their dreams, visions and revelations. Even the church offerings doubled and one of the small churches handed in 6,000 francs for their 6-month offering – and that was after building their new church! All this was accomplished when the power of the Holy Spirit changed the people's lives.'

CHAPTER 9: Dreams and Visions

'Your old men shall dream dreams, Your young men shall see visions.'[53]

The Shell God

My Dad was a doer. He received a calling to be a missionary to the Congo at the tender age of 8 years. After that, he set his face to achieve that goal. By the time he was 12, he was already the church organist and Bible class teacher. When World War II began in 1939, he was assisting his father, regularly preaching in the North Wingfield Assembly as a very young man. Each evening after work, he would study hard for his Bible Correspondence Course. He was then asked to oversee a small church in Carr Vale (near Bolsover). Conscious of his youthful looks, he started growing a moustache to help him to look a little older than his 20 years. Before long he found himself pastoring the Belper Assembly in Derbyshire, followed by a spell as pastor in Willington, County Durham. All these assignments were designed to prepare him for missionary work. Meantime he made sure that he developed all the various practical skills that he

---

[53] Joel 2:28b

would need to be able to maintain cars, build houses, churches, schools and teach.

This does not mean that my father did not have a vision. Without a vision, people perish.[54]

WALTER: *'This was the first vision that God gave to me.'*

'God called me to be a missionary to the Congo when I was only 8 years old.'

'I had already committed my life to Jesus on the railway crossings at North Wingfield in Derbyshire on the way to my first Communion Service. Normally, I would have gone to the Methodist Sunday School as usual, but when we arrived there, my class had been cancelled that morning at the very last minute. With no other option, Mam bundled me into my coat again and took me with her instead to the newly opened Assemblies of God Church that she had begun attending. On the way there she warned me not to take the bread and wine as I had not yet given my heart to Jesus.'

'"*But I want to!*" I said, with all the earnestness in my heart.'

'So my mother gently bent over me alongside the crossings and with tears running down her cheeks, she prayed a simple prayer for me to repeat, asking Jesus to forgive me of anything wrong I had

---

[54] Proverbs 29:18 - 'Where there is no vision, the people perish: but he that keepeth the law, happy is he.' KJV

done, and asking Him to come into my heart and be the Lord of my life. I was 7 years old then.'

'A year later, we had a visiting evangelist come to preach at the North Wingfield Assembly. He invited anyone who wanted prayer to receive the gift of the Holy Spirit as happened to the disciples on the Day of Pentecost[55]. I was already on the front row sitting on my Mam's lap, since the place was full to the brim - every seat taken. My hand shot up and the evangelist laid his hands on me first. Instantly, God filled me with His Spirit and I began to speak in other tongues at the top of my voice for over two hours. By then, the speaker had been round the whole congregation, so his attention turned to this little boy on the front row again, sitting on his mother's knee.'

'In that moment God spoke to him clearly as he saw me lost in the wonderment of God's love and grace. He put his hands on my head again but this time he prayed, *"Father, make this lad a missionary for the Belgian Congo!"* From that moment, my path in life was set and my vision clear; I was going to be a missionary.'

'Nevertheless, God's Word must always be confirmed and the enemy of our souls had his own design on my life. I was doing well at school academically and was also very athletic, having been selected to swim and dive for the Derbyshire County Team. Like my father, I was very good at football too and could have made quite a career for myself in that line. Meantime, my musical skills were

---

[55] Acts 2:1-4

blossoming and at 12 years of age I was already the organist in North Wingfield AoG Church and so was attending every meeting.'

'But my mother knew my true calling was not in sport, so she discouraged me from progressing in that direction. I had already begun to preach at the church, despite being so young, and was teaching the boy's Bible Class in Sunday School. It became quite a dilemma for me: sport, music or the mission field? My school teachers were badgering me to join several teams that would have occupied my Sunday mornings and many evenings. I had to make a choice.'

'Then God himself stepped in. One night He gave me a clear vision. I saw myself tramping down an overgrown path, fording a shallow river and then climbing steadily up a path on the other side towards a village. In front of me was a man leading the way but I saw only his back. When we reached the village, I saw a group of thatched huts clustered around a central sandy area that looked a bit like a street. In front of the first hut there was a tiny thatched structure made of shells and on the door of the hut, I clearly saw an artefact made of shells.'

'In my dream, I asked my guide, "*What is that?*"'

'He replied, "*It's a shell god. The natives worship it*".'

'Immediately, I knew I was in the Congo. Then the vision faded.'

'I sensed that God had spoken to me through that dream and it helped to focus my mind. However, it was not until many years later, when I had just turned 28 years of age, that I revisited the vision. I had joined the Congo Evangelistic Mission a few months earlier when I was 27. It was then that I found myself stationed on the same mission as the evangelist who had prayed over me all those years before!'

'One day, he took me on a missions trip into the bush and I found myself following him down an overgrown path, over a shallow river, stepping carefully along the huge boulders of the ford, then up the other side towards a village.'

'Suddenly, I gasped. **There, in front of us was that very same hut that I had seen in my vision as a 12-year-old lad!** Every detail was the same; the thatched shell structure and the shell artefact hanging by the door. **I looked at the missionary as he strode on ahead of me; yes, he was dressed exactly the same as the man in my dream!**'

'I asked the missionary, "*What is this structure and what does it mean?*" I pointed to the miniature hut.'

'He told me, "*It's a shell house. The natives worship their ancestral spirits whom they believe live in it and they bring them food offerings to appease them.*" I looked more carefully and noticed some broken gourd bowls littered about the area.

'"*And what is this?*" I pointed to the shell artefact dangling by the hut door.'

"It's a shell god," he replied.

"What's that for?" I asked.'

"It's a kind of fertility god," he explained. *"They worship it."*

'I was dumbfounded. My vision had come to pass before my very eyes. **It was the clearest indication to me that I was exactly in the place where God wanted me to be.**'

The Knife

We are all familiar with the Christmas story of how Mary gave birth to Jesus in Bethlehem and how some time later the Magi ('wise men') came to seek out the new king whose star they had seen in the east.[56] They had assumed that the baby would be born in a palace, so they went first of all to see King Herod, which put the life of the child born to be king in danger. After the Magi had found baby Jesus and had given him their prophetic gifts, Joseph was warned in a dream to take his wife Mary and the baby and flee to Egypt in order to escape the ensuing massacre of all the babies in the region of Bethlehem.

God still warns people in dreams and visions today. There may not be anything as drastic as a massacre to escape from but no matter how trivial the circumstances, God cares about every aspect of our lives enough to warn us of impending danger where

---

[56] Matthew 2

necessary, or to reveal unknown facts to us, as He did in Grandma's case:

⟡

LOTTIE: *'Walter was working hard to make a living.'*

'During the miner's strike of 1928, my husband, Walter, found himself out of work. Our pastor, A.C. Colliss, had a herd of milking cows so Walter arranged to purchase milk from him to start a milk round near where we lived. People used to bring their jugs to the door and Walter would fill them up from his churn. This milk round saw us through the worst of the deprivation caused by the strike.'

'At that time, I had made a very good friend called Polly and I often used to call to see her. We used to share many of our experiences and help each other out when we could. Times were extremely hard in those days and we each needed all the support we could get.'

'One day, I found out that someone was spreading malicious rumours that Walter's milk round was not really his but was owned by A.C. Colliss. The inference was that whenever Walter took payment for the milk he had delivered, he was taking money that belonged to our Pastor. As a devout Christian, to have his integrity questioned like this was a great shock and distress to my husband. His reputation in the locality was at stake. People might stop buying his milk or at least find this an excuse to stop paying him for it … and then how would we make ends meet?'

'Of course, I immediately took this dilemma to God in prayer. Then the Lord gave me a vision. I saw a kitchen table and, on the table, a knife. It was a strange, curved knife - very ugly to look at. I had never seen such a curiously shaped knife before. The sight of it filled me with fear. Was someone going to try to kill one of us?'

'The next day I decided to go and share the vision with my friend, Polly. I thought that perhaps she might have some idea what the vision might mean. Mostly, I needed some reassurance and comfort. As I entered her kitchen I met with a sudden shock that stopped me in my tracks: for lying on the table was the very same ugly, curved knife as I had seen in my vision the night before. Shivers ran up my spine and I had to swallow hard in disbelief.'

'Immediately I asked the Lord what it meant. Was I in danger? The reply came directly into my heart: *"There's your answer,"* God said. *"She's the one."* I knew what He meant. Unbeknown to me, my best friend Polly was the one who had been spreading malicious rumours about my husband, trying to discredit him in the community. I couldn't believe it. How could she do this to us? Naturally, I didn't share any of my concerns with her after that.'

'However, it wasn't long before the truth came out in public. Our pastor A.C. Colliss heard of the rumours and put things right by confirming to everyone that Walter was paying him for the milk he supplied and that it was indeed Walter's milk round, so he was entitled to take payment for the milk he delivered to people's doors. My husband was totally exonerated.'

'I think that God gave me the vision to warn me that my best friend was not to be trusted. It was a hard lesson but it taught me that God sees into people's hearts and motives. He knows what is going on and He protects His children from harm, even when they cannot see the danger with their own eyes.'

The Torrent

Like many who were warned through dreams in the Bible[57], my father also had an important dream in 1958 when he was at Kabongo Mission Station in the Congo:

WALTER: *'I'm not normally a dreamer.'*

'When we were missionaries, we left England, our home and our parents behind. Our relatives were very precious to us but we had to leave them in order to fulfil God's call on our lives.'

'About the middle of our third term in Africa, one night I couldn't sleep and I got down beside the bed and was astonished because I saw my father as clearly as I ever saw him. There was my father, Walter Hawkins Senior – he wasn't beside me – he was submerged in what seemed to be a fast-flowing river with his arms around a big rock.'

---

[57] Numbers 12:6 – "If there is a prophet among you, *I*, the LORD, make Myself known to him in a vision; I speak to him in a dream."

'As I watched in horror, I could hear my Dad say, *"Father in Heaven, I've only one son and he's in Africa. I want to see him again. Please let me see my lad again."*'

'Immediately I knew there was something wrong with my Dad and I prayed in desperate earnest for his safety. I couldn't do anything from where I was, but God could do the impossible.'

The following morning, I couldn't get up early enough. I wrote to my mother a long airmail letter saying, *"What are you hiding from me Mam – what is it?"*

'My mother got the letter a week later. Bless her, she used to write an aerogram every week faithfully and I would write a letter back; the whole process would take about a fortnight.'

'This time she wrote back to me saying, *"Son, I don't know how it happened, but I didn't want to burden you. You have your work cut out in Africa. You've such a tremendous burden there at Kabongo, building schools and travelling around the villages, I didn't want to tell you that your Dad was very poorly. He'd been having terrible pain so they got him to the hospital and opened him up. He's still in hospital gravely ill. Do pray for us. Your Dad's been through a very severe illness."*'

'Of course, Hilda and I got straight down on our knees in prayer.'

'Immediately afterwards I saw another vision. I don't normally have visions. I don't have significant dreams or anything like that, but when it's real, I know it.'

'I saw my Dad again, not in the river, but this time in his chair at home and he was looking up at me and holding his stomach in a bear hug.'

'In my vision he said, *"Thank God! Thank God, I've no more pain,"* and I knew it, before my mother could even write to me telling me that he was better, because he had told me so in my dream, *"Thank God, I've no more pain."'*

Walter with his father Walter Hawkins (Snr)

'What a relief it was to me. I wrote back to my mother. I said, *"I've seen this last night in my dream... is this right?"'*

'Mother wrote back and said, "*Yes. There he was, the very time that you saw it, he was sitting in the chair by our fireside and he was holding himself across his tummy, and he said, "Thank God, I've no more pain.""*"'

'Hallelujah! When you're really in touch with God, He can speak to you. But you've got to get that relationship with God in the first place.'

The Glowing Dagger

So far, I have only had one waking vision in my life. It happened in 1998 when my husband and I were on holiday visiting our special friend, Musti, and his family.

Three years previously, my daughters Karen and Claire had bought us our first foreign holiday since our honeymoon in 1988. In the interim, we had been busy bringing up 5 children and had no cash to spare for holidays. So it was such a joy to us when the girls decided to each give us £200 out of their very first wages, saying, "*Mum, you and Mick deserve a holiday.*"

Excitedly, we had searched all possibilities and had found a 2-week unspecified holiday somewhere in Turkey. Bags packed, and a flight to Turkey later, we waited in suspense at the airport to discover where we would be heading. We were allocated a seat on a dusty coach and off we set, still not knowing our destination.

Eventually, we rounded a hill and saw before us a large number of flat-roofed white buildings nestled in the distance around a bay, which we were told was Bodrum. The coach turned left and began to lurch down a very dusty track until it stopped suddenly next to a huge pile of logs; it felt as if we were in the middle of nowhere. Two names were called out, and a couple alighted from the coach, looking around in disbelief. The driver unloaded their luggage, pointed them in the direction of a tin shack and off we set again, lurching down the hillside. *"Poor folks,"* we thought. We began to dread where we might end up!

The next stop found us staring through an arched gateway into a most gorgeous resort; the stuff of every holiday-maker's dreams. A large pool was glistening in the sunshine, begging us to dive in. Then our names were called; this was **our** destination! We were the only ones privileged to leave the coach at that resort and our bags were taken to the reception as if we were royalty.

"What had we done to deserve all this?" we wondered. We realised it must be God's favour. We were taken by the staff to the very best upstairs apartment; the one used in their brochures, overlooking the pool.

That evening, we wandered for miles it seemed around Bodrum bay. As usual, Mick was only interested in finding a guitar shop and we had found nothing except a record shop. He was very disappointed as we stopped at the end of the bay, tired and hungry. *"What had we come to?"* we wondered, sadly.

I spun around, hand on hip, and then let out a scream.

"Mick! A guitar ... I can see a guitar!"

"Where?" he asked.

I pointed. There, through an open doorway leading into the cutest little whitewashed establishment, was a guitar perched on the padded bench at the back. We could so easily have missed it if I hadn't needed to go to the toilet at the end of the pier; we had nearly turned back to climb the hill to our apartment, totally disillusioned with our holiday so far.

Immediately we both ran full pelt towards the guitar; we must have looked quite ridiculous, the pair of us, acting like children who've just spotted a sweetie shop! We burst inside and no one was there apart from the barman. Mick asked about the guitar and the barman explained that a band was playing later. Out of breath, I informed the barman that Mick was a guitarist and without any more ado, he handed the guitar to Mick and asked him to play.

He didn't need to ask Mick twice; Mick swept up the guitar like a long-lost friend, plugged it in and shredded along to the Eric Clapton song that was playing in the background. It was the first time that he had heard that particular song, but he must have made enough of an impression for the barman to invite him to join the band later that evening.

That is how we met Musti. He was the bass player in the 'No Name' band and we became firm friends. We still communicate via email and on Facebook.

Several visits to Turkey later, we spent the last evening of our final trip sharing a barbeque in the back garden at Musti's parent's house in Izmir (modern day Smyrna, of biblical fame), since they lived near to the airport. We had a wonderful time sharing stories of our lives and playing music. Musti's whole family were fantastic musicians; his father played the sazz in the Turkish National Orchestra; his younger brother, Yowuz, played trumpet and keyboards, then his older brother, Gengis, was an amazing guitarist specialising in classical music; finally his oldest brother, Ali, played clarinet. What a family and what a feast!

During the evening, we found out that Ali and his wife, Elvon, had been trying to conceive a baby for many years; they had been through every fertility treatment they could find, without success, and had more or less given up hope. We felt very sad for them, so we offered to pray.

Can you imagine the scene? We all held hands in a circle warmed by the barbeque embers and first Mick prayed out loud and then I prayed, both being careful to pray to *"Our dear Heavenly Father God"* whom we could share. You should have seen their faces – none of them had realised that you could pray openly and simply to God like that, or that we as Christians would be prepared to pray openly for them, being Muslims. They were all stunned and thrilled, and so were we.

That night, we were put in the front lounge on a sofa bed, next to the window. I awoke to hear the Mussulman calling his first prayers of the day. The curtains were swaying gently and I could see the street light outside.

Suddenly as I was gazing at the soft glow of the street light, a strange thing happened; a brilliant cerise-pink object began to poke through the curtain. As I watched, horrified, the object continued to emerge slowly into the room, with the fabric of the curtain closing around it.

I blinked hard and then blinked again even harder. The call to prayer was still sounding across the still night air. There was not a sound in the house apart from my husband's gentle breathing as he slept. I could not take my eyes from the vision and I really could not understand what was happening.

Very gradually, the glowing pink object emerged from the curtain and I could see then that its structure appeared as a single rose on its stem. I was curious. It was the size of a real rose, with translucent cerise pink petals that glowed from within like a precious gem. I then saw that the stem was darker; greenish in colour but still glowing.

Again, I blinked heavily, but the vision did not fade. The rose continued to advance slowly to a point about 4-5 feet above my face until it stopped. I watched the vision intently, trying to take in each detail, when gradually the shape of the rose began to alter, very slightly at first and then more obviously until the rose was no longer a flower but the shape of a feather with the stem as its quill. However, the glowing colour remained the same translucent cerise pink with dark glowing stem.

My mind was whirring; what could this mean? The vision seemed to continue for quite some time as a feather hovering above me, when suddenly, the feather transformed into a glowing dagger with gleaming handle and it shot towards me at an alarming pace.

I screamed, "*Jesus!*" and the dagger stopped abruptly in its tracks about 1 foot away from my nose. Then very slowly the dagger backed out of the curtain at the same point where the rose had emerged. The vision had ended but it left me in turmoil, my heart pounding.

The more I thought about it, the more I realised that the vision was a warning. This was our fourth visit to Turkey in 3 years and each time, we had noticed that our relationship with the band, whilst still extremely precious to us, was perhaps not quite as intense for them. Obviously, they would meet many, many tourists during each holiday season and no doubt they had made many friends before we came along. To us, of course, it was different; Musti, Gokhan, Emin, Sami and the others had become our very dear Turkish friends.

Even so, Musti called Mick his brother and we called his parents "*Baba*" (Dad) and "*Anneh*" (Mum). "*Meeek*," he would say,

"*You are my brudder.*" To this day, he remains our beloved Turkish brother.

However, my vision has warned us not to return to Turkey; we have experienced the rose and the feather. We don't want to find out what the dagger meant.

As a happy sequel to this event, exactly a year later we received a very excited telephone call from Musti. "*Meeek*," he said, "*God has answered your prayer. Elvon has had a baby boy and he is perfect and doing well.*"

We were thrilled. That was yet another miracle of God's grace. She had conceived the baby naturally, after having given up hope when all the fertility treatments failed. Praise God!

CHAPTER 10: Miracle Workers

'We are ordinary people connected to a supernatural God therefore we can expect to do extraordinary things for Him.' Ps. PAUL GEERLING[58]

Having been brought up in Pentecost, it is easy to accept the supernatural as normal in church life. Firstly, we hear of all the miracles Jesus performed, then we read Scriptures such as, *'... greater works than these he will do, because I go to my Father.'*[59]

But when we ourselves are faced with circumstances requiring a miracle, it's not so easy to be blasé. Here are accounts of some miracle-workers whom I have met and admired over the years, starting with an Aussie evangelist who is larger than life but who has had to prove God again and again in his ministry.

Tim Hall

Tim Hall makes an almost yearly pilgrimage to Hope City Church in Sheffield, being one of Pastor David Gilpin's mentors and a great friend of the church.[60]

---

[58] Together with his wife (Jo), co-pastor of iSEE CHURCH, a multisite church originating in Australia.

[59] John 14:12

[60] Correct at the time Pearl wrote this. As of 2024, Dave and Jenny Gilpin now live on the Gold Coast of Australia.

In the *Fabulous Conference 2009*, Tim Hall preached an amazing sermon about Jesus entitled '*Mr Fabulous*'. In it, he recalled that when preaching one Sunday morning in a church in Papua New Guinea, a man was brought in on a stretcher. The poor guy was in a foetal position and terribly grey-looking with horrible cancerous growths on his feet. Tim did not dare to look at the guy throughout the service, dreading what was surely to come; he would be expected to pray for this spectre of a man, who was barely conscious and obviously near to death.

After preaching, Tim did what only Tim does best, which is to invite God to move in healing power among the people. He prayed over the whole congregation, getting everyone to lay hands on any afflicted part of their own body and then he encouraged them to move the ailing limb, or feel if lumps had disappeared, or feel if the pain had gone.

In the commotion that followed, the foetal man rolled over and fell off his stretcher. Then amazingly he stood up in faith on his massive tumours. At this, Tim felt boldness surge through him and he went over and prayed for the man. At that moment, the man's feet went bang flat on the floor - the tumours had all but disappeared in an instant. Tim couldn't believe his eyes!

That evening, there was a terrible cyclone and the stewards were furiously bailing out the stadium. There was chaos in the place – not the sort of holy atmosphere in which you might imagine that God would move in such miraculous power. But in Tim's own words, the man who had been taxied in on a stretcher *"walked across the stage as if he was entering the Olympics – totally healed!"*

Later, Tim Hall told us of a man in New Zealand whose arm had been severed and was hanging off. The medics had stitched him up but all his tendons were severed. When Tim prayed for him, the fingers began to grow and his arm was healed.

As Tim explained in his message about Jesus, *"Mr. Fabulous is the flashing effulgence of the express image of God by whom He stamped His image on all human flesh ... If you want knowledge, it's all in Him. Jesus upholds every system on the earth and in the universe. He made all things by the word of His power. He is before all things."* ... *"I want to know Him intimately,"* Tim added. ***"We tiny specs can be carriers of the power of God."***

Harold & Josie Womersley

I first remember meeting Harold Womersley, his beautiful wife, Josie, their teenage son, David, and daughter, Patsy, in 1954 when he was already a silver-haired veteran. I would be 4 years old, coming with my parents Walter and Hilda Hawkins to join Harold and Josie at Kabongo mission station. My father was due to take over from the Womersleys whilst they returned to England for a much-needed furlough.

In 1924, Harold Womersley was among the first intrepid missionaries to enter the Congo to join the Congo Evangelistic

Mission started by William F.P. Burton and James Salter in 1915. He and his two companions, Edmund (Teddy) Hodgson and Norman Effemy, had to travel for eight weeks by steamer, train and river boat, then trek mile after mile in the scorching heat to reach Mwanza, the first mission station to be built in the Katanga region nine years previously. At that time, the only other occupied missions were at Ngoimani and Kipushya. When they reached Kigomo en route to Mwanza, Teddy and Harold took a detour and trudged five miles to Ujiji out of respect to see the famous mango tree that marked the spot where Henry Morton Stanley raised his cap and said, *"Doctor Livingstone, I presume."*[61]

On his very first Sunday in the Congo, Harold Womersley took his violin and followed Willie Burton to a village 3 miles away from Mwanza to hold an open-air meeting. He was so frustrated that he could not speak the Kiluba language but at least he could attract a crowd with his violin playing. That evening he witnessed his very first bonfire meeting in the village at the foot of Mwanza hill with hundreds of pairs of eyes gleaming in the darkness and hundreds of voices chanting and singing heartily their praise to God. After Willie Burton preached the gospel, a native evangelist's wife stood up to testify. She told everyone that she had been suffering for 2 months with an agonising leg condition that had become so painful and twisted that she could not walk. When she could bear the pain no more, she and her husband cried out to God to heal her. Now her leg

---

[61] This mango tree eventually fell and was replaced by a monument.

was perfectly well and strong; God had wonderfully healed her. The crowd burst into noisy celebration but the evangelist's wife called for quiet. She had more to say. *"My heart was once even more twisted than my leg,"* she confessed. *"I'm too ashamed to say exactly what my terrible sin was but I do know this, that He who straightened out my leg, straightened out my heart also."* Then she stared round at all the eyes gleaming in the firelight and fixed their gaze. *"Won't you come and believe on the same wonderful Saviour? He can do the same for you, too!"*

The following morning after attending the sunrise prayer meeting, Harold was finally given the opportunity to unpack his bags in his temporary quarters. Then Willie Burton proudly showed Harold the kiln where he had been firing sun-dried bricks made of anthill clay with the instructions that since Harold had been an apprentice builder for one year in England, he was to start at once and build a fireproof office for Mwanza mission. Meantime his travelling companion Teddy Hodgson left immediately for Kisanga to re-establish Jimmy Salter's old mission station there.

Thus, Harold started laying foundations with a trowel in one hand and a sheet of Kiluba building phrases in the other so that he could communicate with his African helpers. To erect the building, he first had to fell suitable trees, teach the Africans to saw them into planks for the framework and learn how to make his own bricks and mortar. The roof had to be constructed using poles trimmed from the trunks of sturdy saplings in the forest and covered with Kipamba grass thatch. To make this as fireproof as possible, Mr. Burton's idea was to construct a nine-inch-thick clay ceiling over the office to delay any fire long enough for the place to be evacuated.[62] For additional fire and sun protection, the ceiling was to extend 3 feet from the external walls in all directions, supported by arched pillars to form a veranda. Harold soon realised that this job was a lot harder than he had bargained for and it gave him a whole new perspective on the Bible narrative when God confused the language of the builders of the Tower of Babel. He was having the same problems with his native workers! His sheet of helpful phrases was limited to things like, *"Throw up that half brick!"* or *"Don't stop work yet, bricks are needed here!"*

Only 3 months after arriving in the Congo, Harold took the plunge and preached a simple message in the morning service in Kiluba. He had been studying the language for hours every day and felt proud of his accomplishment until one of the Africans told him with a broad grin, *"Well, missionary, we haven't understood a word you've said, but of course a child must crawl before it can walk!"*

This was Harold Womersley's introduction to missionary life. There followed over 50 years of faithful service as a missionary for which Harold Womersley received the prestigious Belgian accolades

---

[62] Years later that ceiling was nearly the death of Willie Burton when, without any warning, it suddenly collapsed. Fortunately, Mr. Burton dived under his desk just in time as the heavy ceiling crashed around him, from where he was eventually rescued very badly shaken. It appeared that termites had completely eaten away the ceiling supports!

of Chevalier de l'Ordre de Leopold II and Chevalier de l'Ordre du Lion in recognition of his services to the Congo.

CHAPTER 11: Lightning Bolts

'You can live dangerously because God loves you.'

Ps. DAVID JOHN MACPHAIL[63]

Kabondo Dianda

It was a shock in more ways than one when my parents landed in Africa as rookie missionaries in November 1944. Little could have prepared them for the ferocious tropical storms that were almost daily occurrences during the rainy season between September and March. One minute, the earth would be shimmering under a blistering midday sun and then out of nowhere a handful of tiny cotton wool clouds would suddenly combine, burgeoning upwards into menacing thunderheads. After a few warning rumbles, the light show would start in earnest, preceding a torrent of heavy rain or sometimes even hail the size of golf balls. The storm might last for only an hour or so and then disappear as quickly as it had arrived leaving welcome pools of collected rainwater for the animals to drink, some broken branches here and there, perhaps a smouldering

---

[63] Together with his wife, Karen, David John ('DJ') is the Senior Pastor of Liberty Church, Randburg, South Africa.

tree that had suffered a direct hit, and more often than not a few fatalities in the villages along its path.

After a storm had passed, I used to love the sultry smell of damp earth mingled with the heady scents of tropical blooms and the spicy, pungent aroma of tree bark. You could see a blanket of steam rising to meet the last fading clouds as they were rapidly burnt off under the searing blaze of the equatorial sun and within minutes the whole landscape would appear as parched as ever. The abruptness of this process was like watching a dog plunge into a stream, paddle around for a minute or two and then clamber out, shaking the water from its coat and hey presto! – dry again as if nothing had happened.

The mission station at Kabondo Dianda was first pioneered by Teddy Hodson and Garfield Vale in the 1920s. Garfield stayed on there to build the church and first mission house. He used to go around the local village and call everyone into the church every Sunday morning, including the old chief Kabondo Dianda. Now chiefs in those days were a demagogic force to be reckoned with and were greatly feared by their subjects. It was therefore very brave of Garfield Vale to dare to approach this man without the usual formalities required if one wanted to sleep safe in one's bed at night! Yet over the years, a rapport was achieved and mutual respect garnered from the sheer persistence of this early pioneer missionary.

Garfield was replaced by Cyril and Frances Yessen at Kabondo Dianda in 1937. My parents, Walter and Hilda Hawkins, later joined them there in early 1945 to replace them so that they could eventually return to England in mid-1945 on furlough.

Many years later the old chief's son, the new chief Kabondo Dianda, gave my father a beaded ceremonial spear that we have in our possession to this day. Dad preached to this chief many times in his compound and challenged him to repent and give his life to Jesus Christ.

Frances' Near Escape

WALTER: *'Frances was a miracle woman that day.'*

'Hilda and I finally arrived at our very first Congo mission station in January 1945 after 10 weeks of gruelling travel under war conditions. We were greeted by Cyril and Frances Yessen, the senior missionaries at Kabondo Dianda mission station. Whilst we had yet to establish ourselves and were given a broken-down hovel to live in, the Yessens were comfortably living in the main mission house. Kabondo Dianda was a sheet of rock – our houses were built on it and this attracted lots of lightning strikes. Within a couple of months of our arrival there was a massive tropical storm.'

'The main mission house had a central corridor under the roof ridge, with rooms leading off on both sides. Frances had just walked down the corridor towards the side entrance door to see what was happening outside. She had her hand on the handle to open the door when the lightning struck. The lightning bolt followed the wall on her left until it reached the point where she stood. It ricocheted over her head from that wall and blew a hole in the wall a foot wide to her right into the kitchen. It crossed the kitchen, hit the outer wall where it left a big hole and buried itself into the ground. It was a miracle that Frances escaped death that day.'

Kabongo

My parent's third stint as missionaries in central Africa was spent at Kabongo, a place very dear to my heart. We had far more facilities at Kabongo Mission Station compared to our earlier homes in the Congo, which made the place seem luxurious to a child like myself who had experienced little of the world beyond the austere rigours of missionary life. For example, we had a choice of two toilets, each housed in its own little whitewashed hut well away from the main building. Okay, the toilet seat was only a wooden box with a hole in the top, positioned above a cesspit that was deep enough to keep the cockroaches from nibbling one's delicate parts! And, we had scraps of paper torn from old letters, envelopes and suchlike that Mum threaded onto a piece of string to serve as toilet paper. This was much better than having to use leaves!

I'll never forget one particular day when I called my mother to go to the toilet with me (we always went to the toilet in convoy because of the risk of attack by predators and other such dangers lurking along the pathway). Fortunately, it was Mum who opened the ramshackle door on this occasion. She couldn't understand why it was so resistant so she pushed harder and then poked her head around the door only to find herself eyeball to eyeball with a massive black mamba! With a shriek, she slammed the door shut and nearly fell over me in her panic to escape.

"*Nyoka! Nyoka!*" she screamed and I knew all too well what that meant: "*Snake!*" I ran ahead of my mother to get help and very soon my father was on the scene with rifle in hand, followed by everyone else who had heard the commotion. Very cautiously, my father eased the door open only to find that the snake was disappearing rapidly down the hole in the middle of the toilet seat! Dad just had time to whack the snake with the butt of his rifle before it disappeared. Weren't we glad that we had two toilets then! Of course, my father couldn't leave a 20-foot deadly snake at the bottom of our toilet, even if it did have its back broken, so with the help of one of our native staff, he lowered a kerosene lamp down the hole and eventually managed to shoot the snake dead. What a relief that was! However, we still couldn't use that toilet for over three months because of the terrible smell of rotting snake flesh. If you've never smelled a dead snake, you haven't missed much. There is no more pungent, acrid, loathsome stench that I have ever come across in all my life.

Talking of luxuries, we also had a bathroom with a concrete sink and fixed bath, both fed from a large external brick water butt that had an open hearth under the tank for heating the water.

Obviously, we depended largely on an adequate rainfall to fill the water tank and bath nights had to be planned well in advance to ensure that the water was hot, but nevertheless this arrangement was far superior than having to fill a tin tub with cold water from the river, not to mention the risk of encountering a crocodile or hippopotamus en route! We did have fun with our plumbing, however. One night, when I was enjoying a lovely hot soak in the bath, suddenly the plug popped up and before I could move an inch, a tiny long-nosed elephant mouse was swimming beside me. It was as frantic to get out of the bath as I was and it tried to scramble up my leg! Yes, more screaming followed ... in fact I think that I must have screamed a lot as a child when I remember all the encounters I had with strange creatures of all kinds! I recall another memorable bath time at school in Sakeji, Zambia when I turned the tap on only to find that instead of water, a stream of red centipedes cascaded out and filled the bath until it was completely full to overflowing with a writhing mass of inch-long creepy crawlies! They must have bred in the water tank and drunk all the water dry. We couldn't have a bath for weeks after that!

My father was very resourceful and at Kabongo he managed to rig up a few basic electric lights so that we could read at night instead of having to go to bed when the sun set at 6pm. I guess you could call it a *gentle glow* that was produced rather than *light*, possibly equivalent to a 20-watt bulb. The electricity was sourced from a small generator that we affectionately called Tiny Tim. What a luxury this was! Before this innovation, we used to have to manage with candles, paraffin lamps and torches.

In fact, my father had to be a 'Jack of all trades', never more so than when our station vehicle needed major repairs, which proved to be quite often because of the treacherous roads and tracks that he had to drive along. Sometimes, the roads would be flooded with torrential rain and for days afterwards would be like a quagmire and totally impassable. At other times, the sun would bake the road surface into mountainous ridges and grooves, deep pits and hollows that would sheer back axles or tear at the undercarriage with disastrous effect. There were no garages or repairmen to call on, so Dad had to become fairly proficient at making do and mending all sorts of things.

With this in mind, at Kabongo we actually had the luxury of our own garage and a special pit dug into the floor so that essential repairs could be attempted. The garage was next to Dad's office in a building separated from the main house by a gently sloping sandy area about the size of a football pitch. This vast empty space served many purposes, not only as a parade ground when the children in our mission school had anything to celebrate, or a place where malnourished mothers who had lost their milk came to queue for reconstituted milk to feed their babies, or even as a playground for lonely me, but most of all it was a vital firebreak in case of bush fires. Very often these fires were caused by lightning strikes and both the thunder storms and the fire storms that they espoused were among the most terrifying phenomena that we had to face in the Congo.'

'Almost every time that an electric storm passed over, we would hear of some tragedy in a local village. In particular, the many tiny villages bordering Lake Boya (Mushroom Lake) in the valley beyond our mission station were particularly subject to lightning strikes and every year someone was killed in these settlements. The lake seemed to attract lightning like a magnet and during the six months of the wet season, electric storms were a frequent occurrence, so the death toll would grow and the misery pile up for the villagers. It was during one such storm that my father's life was suddenly on the line as he worked on his truck in the garage pit. It was a pure miracle that he survived:

Dad's Bolt from the Blue

WALTER: *'It came from nowhere.'*

'My best companion at Kabongo was Capiteni, who was not only a terrific Christian but also a very practical man. He used to assist me with most of my projects around the mission station such as house building and car repairs.'

'One memorable day in 1956 during our first rainy season at Kabongo, I decided to look at the brakes and back axle of the red Chevrolet camionette that I had inherited as our mission vehicle. It was hot, clammy weather and I was glad of the excuse to climb into the cool shelter of the garage pit so that I could get underneath the vehicle to tackle the repairs. I had noticed that rain was on the way from the clouds burgeoning over the horizon but as yet no distant thunder or lightning could be heard. There would be plenty of time before the downpour arrived. In any case, the garage was well protected by my office to the right and a storehouse to the left, with strong timber beams overhead supporting the tin roof.'

'All seemed well as I took a selection of tools with me for the job. Capiteni helped me wherever he could and the refit was progressing apace. I had nearly completed the re-assembly of the rear end parts when I realised that I needed a $\frac{3}{8}$" spanner to tighten the last nuts.'

'"*Pass me that spanner over there,*" I called to Capiteni in his native language Kiluba. I indicated which size I required and when Capiteni had found it, he stooped down to pass it to me under the vehicle. I grasped the tool firmly and then it happened. A tremendous flash focussed on my office. The whole area filled with sizzling, pent up energy. Suddenly, I was tingling with it and became the conductor. Then an explosive blast hit me that passed along my arm in an agonising surge, binding my hand to the spanner. The metal tool linked me to Capiteni and he was lifted off the ground, spinning like a top, until he fell writhing to the ground. At that instant I thought we were both done for. Millions of volts had just passed through my body, along the spanner and into my dear friend.'

'It took me a while to gather my senses and even longer to be able to let go of my grip on the spanner. I shouted to Capiteni and after a fearful delay, at last I heard him groan softly. Thank God, he was unhurt! He was alive and so was I! It was a miracle. We should have both been electrocuted by such a massive dose of electricity. It had been a shot out of the blue, literally. One moment, the sun was shining and the next, before any visible sign of the impending storm had gathered overhead, the lightning bolt had struck.'

'As we staggered out of the garage away from the vehicle and any metal tools, we noticed that the heavy wooden lintel above the office door had been snapped by the lightning bolt. If the strike had the power to split a massive beam of wood, how much more damage could the lightning have done to our poor bodies? Yet, thank God, our lives were spared.'

'Since there was still no sign of rain, we ran across the compound to the mission house for a welcome cup of tea. Hilda, my wife, had heard the blast and was anxiously looking to see if we had been hit by lightning. When we told her what had just happened, we all took the opportunity to get down on our knees and thank our Heavenly Father who so graciously preserved us. Capiteni and I could both have been killed!'

Mum's Near Miss

HILDA: *'Mum and I escaped death by a whisker.'*

'I would have been about 17 years old and still living with my parents and two brothers at our farm in Derbyshire, England. The year was 1936.'

'Chestnuts Farm was a group of stone buildings nestled on the bleak hillside above Bonsall. In parts of the main farmhouse, the walls were almost the thickness of a doorway, so you would have thought them impenetrable to virtually anything.'

'One day a sudden violent storm came over the farm. My oldest brother, Billy, was out at work and my father, William Potter, was in the cowshed tending to the livestock. Oswald, my other brother, was caught out in the open and began to run for cover towards the farmhouse but had no time to get into the house and he had to shelter in an empty pigsty nearby. He heard a massive bang and realised that the house had been struck by lightning, so as soon as he dared to move, he ran in to see if we were alright.'

'My mother, Florrie, and I had been sitting cosily in the kitchen by the open fire when the lightning struck, sending a ball of white light shooting across the room in our direction. Before we could flinch even, the bolt roared through the gap between us with an ear-splitting explosion. Mum had been sitting at the kitchen table and I was sitting by the hearth, keeping warm. We screamed in unison, thrust aside by the force of the blast.'

'Fortunately, there had been a three-foot gap between us and that is precisely where the lightning bolt went to ground on a faulty earth fitting. A scorch mark was all that was left to indicate what had happened. It appeared that an amateur electrician had earthed the rainwater tank supply that came into the kitchen tap onto a lead pipe. The lightning had struck the metal tank and had nowhere to go. It came like a mighty flash with a frightening bang between us and earthed itself via the pipe that fed into the main water tank. If there had not been a gap between us, at least one of us would have died.'

'After the flash, my mother said to me, "*Are you alright?*"'

'"*Yes*," I said, dithering with fright. "*Are you?*"'

'We were both extremely shaken but very grateful to God for sparing our lives, because we could so easily have been in the direct line of that lightning strike. In the Bible, God promises that He will protect us and I have proved this to be true throughout my life. I'm still here to testify to His constant protection over 70 years later!'

CHAPTER 12: Fuel for Thought

'Give me oil in my lamp, keep me burning...'[64]

We are accustomed to the fact that machines require fuel to operate. But what happens if that energy source is no longer available? In the natural order of things, an engine without fuel simply stops working. But in God's economy, this is not always the case. Sometimes the required fuel happens to arrive just when it is needed; on other occasions, the engine carries on operating without any apparent energy source. Either way, such remarkable miracles have happened in my family, to the glory of God.

Dad's Perilous Flight

WALTER: *'Our lives were on the line.'*

'As Missionary Secretary and Director for the British Assemblies of God Missions between 1963 and 1988, it was my privilege to travel overseas many times to care for our workers abroad. On one such journey, God spared my life in a very remarkable way.'

---

[64] From the hymn, 'Sing Hosanna', written by A. Sevison.

'It had been a difficult task to coordinate all the transportation required for an intensive visit to all our missionaries throughout Africa. Fortunately, the Missions Council had nominated my good friend and fellow ex-missionary, John Emmett, to accompany me on the six-week trip during July and August 1984 because he knew the Congo well. At least I would not have to face this journey alone. I arranged that we should start in Sierra Leone for a brief visit to our missionaries there and then transfer to Kinshasa, the capital of Congo, where I was due to address a Graduation Service for many future ministers and evangelists from the American AoG Bible School.'

'From Kinshasa, we took a British Airways flight to Bukavu in north east Congo where we were due to be met by our own AoG pilot for the next stage of our journey in a 5-seater Piper aeroplane. While in Bukavu, I took the opportunity to preach in the Swedish Mission and also visit our General Offices for the north east Congo territory in order to consolidate plans for the erection of a Bible School.'

'It was a real come-down to have to scramble into such a tiny aeroplane after the luxuries of an airliner but I was very excited because we would be flying directly over the four mission stations on which I had lived during my sixteen years as a missionary to the Congo. John, too, had worked with his wife on a neighbouring mission station to ours at one time, so he was just as thrilled as I was. First of all, we were low enough to see Bujumbura Mission and the top of Lake Tanganyika, which is the second deepest lake on

Earth. I pointed out the memorial erected at the very spot where Stanley found Livingstone in the early pioneering days. I explained to John how deeply I had been moved with emotion when I had stood on that hallowed ground as a young missionary. Livingstone's were big boots to fill.'

'We crossed over the lake towards the Congo side where colossal mountains towered into the tropical sky. We spotted Uvira mission, then Baraka and many of our churches such as Lwata, all perched beside the deep waters. In the distance, we could see the winding escarpment road climbing over the heights to Fizi and Lulimba. Swiftly we descended to land in Albertville, now called Kalemie. Our friends were there to sing and welcome us with great warmth. Here I was in my own territory and I was able to speak the language I had mastered and loved, Kiluba.'

'Some of our European friends reminded me of the terrible time 20 years earlier during the Simba uprising, when they had helped me to load two tonnes of food and relief clothing onto a Belgian army lorry to take to the impoverished churches around Lulimba, one hundred miles inland. I had been left overnight with the missionaries at Lulimba Mission Station to distribute the food and clothing to the pastors there, but we were suddenly overtaken by a group of rebels who wanted to steal the provisions. I remembered how a Simba rebel soldier had pushed his bayonet under my chin, threatening to murder me, but when he found that I knew his language, he relented and to my great relief dropped his gun. The next day we had been picked up by a Belgian army truck with an escort for safety on the return journey from the relief mission to Lulimba. We had only travelled three miles along the narrow single-track road when we came to a sudden halt. Right there in front of the vehicle was a massive crater. We had all jumped down to inspect the damage and it was then that we discovered that a bomb had been set in the road by the Simba rebels during the night to catch passing vehicles. A poor cyclist had passed by before we arrived and the bomb had detonated, killing him outright. How grateful we were that God had graciously preserved our lives. It could so easily have been us lying there on the road, mangled and mutilated.'

'After much reminiscing, of good times as well as bad, it was hard to tear ourselves away from the many believers we knew so well in Kalemie. The next part of our flight took us over Katea Mission Station where my companion, John Emmett, had once worked. He was so thrilled to see the place again. We then passed over Kongolo town where my wife, Hilda, and I had pioneered the work. It was there where our precious baby, Pearl, took her first steps and learned to talk in the native language, Kiluba. Our house at Kongolo was a mere 40 yards from the great Congo River where crocodiles and hippos visited us regularly. During the long journey, I told John about the tremendous revival we experienced in Kongolo, with 35 villages opened to the Gospel and 13 churches built in only 13 months. I think he was quite amazed!'

'We stopped to refuel at Kipushya and again at Kamina. Our pilot was obliged to spend some time in Kamina mending a puncture as one of the tyres on the aeroplane was flat. This gave me the opportunity to revisit Kabongo, the last mission station at which I had worked with my wife Hilda between 1954 and 1960. The 90-mile journey north by truck to Kabongo was over rough terrain and unmade roads. John and I stayed a whole week there so that I could see all the various leaders whom I had appointed prior to our hasty evacuation 24 years earlier during the rebel insurgence after Independence in 1960.

I could hardly recognise our old mission house at Kabongo, it was so run down and dilapidated. I slept on a camp bed in my old bedroom. It was tragic to see that the ceiling had collapsed and all that remained overhead was the old corrugated roof. Nevertheless, the place was still standing and I was overjoyed to find that the churches were thriving after the terrible persecution of the intervening years. I had left 143 churches in the region in 1960 and these had now increased to a total of 250 churches. I received so many hugs and shared countless tears of joy with our old friends who came from far and wide throughout the region to greet me. I could scarcely tear myself away from them all and it was with a very heavy heart that I left Kabongo for the last time.'

'Back in Kamina, the waiting 5-seater aeroplane complete with mended tyre flew us to Lubumbashi, formerly Elisabethville, in the south of Shaba Province. There we met John, the intrepid pilot who would share an incredible adventure with us. The Mission Aviation Fellowship had kindly agreed to send John with their 6-seater aeroplane to take us on the rest of our itinerary through Zimbabwe, Mozambique and the Transvaal.

Before us lay a long, gruelling journey down the centre of Africa to Harare the capital of Zimbabwe, where we found that our missionaries were doing a fine work. There were also a number of vocational missionaries called 'Lifeliners' throughout the region, so I gathered them all together for a few days' discussion and fellowship.'

'Ahead lay a flight over the dangerous border into Mozambique to the capital city of Maputo. I remembered how on a previous trip I was taken to speak at a meeting on a farm near the border with Mozambique. Halfway through the service, a loud cry went up and all the men charged out of the room, collecting their guns as they left. I was astounded. Someone told me that invaders from over the border were pillaging the gardens and that the men were rushing off to defend their properties. The atmosphere was tense as we prayed with the women that God would spare the lives of their husbands and sons. We were tremendously relieved when all the men returned half an hour later. No one had been hurt in the conflict but we could sense a belligerent attitude prevailing, which was understandable after so many years of warring and border skirmishes.'

'Our pilot, John, took us east from Harare over the border to Maputo where we held meetings with our missionaries and evangelists in Mozambique. Meantime, the pilot searched for some aviation fuel so that we could continue our journey towards White River where the Emmanuel Press was located. Unfortunately, despite his best efforts, John could find no fuel at all. He was informed that due to acute shortages, every aeroplane arriving in Maputo was expected to have sufficient fuel for the return journey. What a shock!'

'We accompanied John as he anxiously tested his two tanks and we could see clearly that neither registered any fuel at all. He was troubled and afraid to take off, which did not exactly inspire confidence in my companion John Emmett and myself. The pilot explained to us that he had to take a prescribed path between the entrenchments of anti-aircraft missile ranges located along the South African border, which would require more fuel than if we were to fly in a straight line to our destination. The airport staff at Maputo then informed him of a tiny emergency airstrip just over the border at a place called Komartipoort, where they assured him we would be able to find fuel. All the same, we were the ones going up with empty fuel tanks, and we were not at all reassured!'

'The three of us knelt and prayed earnestly for divine help. There seemed little option but to risk taking off for Komartipoort, otherwise we could be stuck in Mozambique indefinitely. We climbed aboard and John the pilot started the engines while John Emmett and I continued to pray fervently. Then we fell silent as the small aeroplane taxied along the runway. I could feel my heart thudding in my chest. At last we became airborne and climbed into the blue sky. The indicators on both fuel gauges were on 'EMPTY'. We prayed all the way to Komartipoort until with enormous relief we alighted abruptly on the rough runway.'

'We were hot, sticky and fairly shaken after our daring flight across the border, but very glad to be alive. Our problems seemed to be over. The three of us strode towards the small terminal building full of hope. Imagine our abject horror when the airport staff at Komartipoort told us that they had no fuel at all and could not help us. Hope turned to dismay. We returned to the tiny aeroplane and surveyed the mountain range that lay between us and Nelspruit Airport, one hundred miles to the east. Our pilot removed each fuel cap in turn and dipped in his dipstick. The result was the same in both tanks; the dipstick remained dry as a bone. Perhaps hoping for a different result, he climbed up and stretched his arm down as far as he could to carefully examine the bottom of each tank with his fingertips; both times his hand came out completely dry.' We looked at each other in despair.

'"*We have no other choice but to try to reach Nelspruit*," John concluded after much debate.'

'"*But what will we do if the engines stop in mid-air?*" I asked.'

'He looked pale. "*I'll just have to try and land on a road*," he replied.'

'I was not convinced. Even if we found a road on which to land, there would very likely be some traffic on it. Then there were the mountains. How could we hope to cross those safely with no fuel in the tanks, assuming that we were able to lift off the ground in the first place? The prospect was totally unacceptable and far too dangerous.'

'There was another, equally sinister problem weighing on my mind. At Nelspruit Airport, there was only a simple uni-directional landing strip at that time, so that aircraft always had to descend one way only, irrespective of which way the wind was blowing. I had bad memories of one of our Lifeline missionary doctors who was attempting to land at Nelspruit Airport in poor weather conditions and he lost control in the cross-wind. His aeroplane crashed, killing his wife outright. That tragedy had shocked us to the core.'

'Pilot John climbed into the cockpit ready for take-off. My remonstrations fell on deaf ears. I could only follow John Emmett grudgingly into the 6-seater, all the while crying out to God to protect our tiny aeroplane and its passengers. I reminded God that we were about His business and I recalled how God had protected my wife Hilda and me from the U-boats when we crossed the Atlantic Ocean in convoy during World War II and how He had protected us on many occasions since then from what could have been certain death.'

'The engines found fuel enough to start, warm up, and take off. I held my breath and clutched my seat in terror as we gained height to cross the mountains. You could cut the atmosphere in the cabin with a knife. My eyes focussed intently on the scene below. It was a peculiar relief to watch the terrain passing by and to hear the continued purring of the engines. Every moment of flight was a bonus. All the time I was talking to God in prayer, recounting His goodness to me and trusting in His mercy to see us safely over the mountain range to Nelspruit.'

'Amazingly, after what seemed a heart-stopping eternity, the airport came into view and we began our gliding descent. John completely ignored the one-way system and dropped down abruptly at the first end of the runway regardless of the possibility of meeting any oncoming aircraft. You could hear our combined sighs of relief over the screeching tyre noise as the breaks were applied. We were safe!

It was an absolute miracle how we could make two journeys spanning well over a hundred miles on empty fuel tanks. We began to laugh and holler with incredulous joy. God had performed an astounding miracle for us; there was no doubt about that! The aeroplane came to a stop on the runway right next to two petrol pumps. With a shout of victory, our pilot John jumped out and climbed up to the filler ports. John Emmett and I clambered down and passed the pipe up to him. John let each tank fill until it was running over, he was so thrilled to have fuel at last for the return journey to Johannesburg.'

'That was truly one of the worst days of my life. Yet through that miracle I have come to realise that God is able to perform astonishing acts, contrary to all-natural expectation, in order to rescue and preserve the lives of His children.'

Grandad's Outing

Dad's remarkable, breath-taking journey was not the only occasion when God stepped in to provide transport for our family. As far back as my grandfather's time, when cars were a novelty and petrol stations were few and far between, God sent fuel to help them reach their destination.

WALTER HAWKINS SENIOR: *'A tanker came up the road.'*

'One summer's day our pastor, Wilfred Colliss, invited my wife Lottie and me to accompany him on an outing from Chesterfield to the Peak District in his newfangled Morris car for a picnic. We were delighted at the prospect as we rarely left North Wingfield where we lived in Derbyshire. In fact, I hardly ever enjoyed much sunlight at all because at the time I used to work in the colliery and spent most of my days deep underground in the mine.'

'We set out in glorious sunshine and climbed slowly up winding lanes into the Peak District. Lottie was so excited, sitting bolt upright like a real lady in a posh car and we were all admiring the stunning views on all sides. I had never seen anywhere so beautiful; the Derwent River winding its way between steep grassy slopes criss-crossed with stone walls and dotted with clusters of contented sheep. Sheer rock formations rose like buttresses from the nursery slopes, each vying with the next for size and breath-taking magnificence. In the valleys were ribbons of cottages perched on various vantage points, each village boasting its own church with tower or spire rising majestically out of dense groves of trees whose leaves were dancing and glistening in the sunlight.'

'Suddenly, in the middle of beyond, the engine began to sputter and the car gradually ground to a halt. Wilfred got out and tried to crank the engine up again but when that failed he returned to the driver's seat and started to tap some of the control dials. All of a sudden he slapped his forehead and groaned as he realised that he had forgotten to fill up with petrol before we set out for the day!'

'We all looked at each other in dismay; we were far from any garage or even a village where we might find someone with a container of fuel. Wilfred knew that in such hilly terrain, there was no prospect of pushing the car more than a few yards at best. It was a hopeless situation. There was not a solitary cottage or farmhouse in sight where we might seek shelter. In those days it was very rare for drivers to pass another automated vehicle on the road, especially in remote parts as we were on that day. It appeared that our happy outing had turned into a disaster.'

'It was then that Wilfred spoke to God in prayer. He said, "O, Father God, will you please help us in this remote area to get the petrol we need? I must get Walter and Lottie back home and we are far in the wilds. Please show us what to do, Lord!"'

'Immediately he had finished praying, he looked through his rear-view mirror and to his amazement he saw that a massive petrol tanker was approaching up the hill and it would soon overtake their stranded car. In a flash, Wilfred jumped out of the car and stood with his hands outstretched to bar the way of the tanker. The driver stopped at once.'

'Wilfred explained our problem but the driver shook his head. *"I'm so sorry,"* he said. *"I can't help you. I've just emptied both sides of the dual tank at a garage a few miles away."'*

"'Can't we see if we can squeeze the last drop out somehow?" queried Wilfred, scarcely able to disguise his disappointment.'

"'No chance of that!" the driver said. *"The garage owners always empty every last dribble out with their buckets so as to get their full money's worth. I'm sorry I can't oblige you, sir."'*

'Wilfred looked dejected. "Isn't there anything we can do?" he asked. Then looking to heaven in sheer desperation, he cried, *"Lord, help us!"'*

"'Well..." The driver cupped his chin in his hand. He had just hit on an idea. On either side of the road were steep banks rising up towards the stone walling at the edge of the adjoining fields. *"We'll give it a try,"* he said without explaining what he was about to do. Straightway he clambered up into the driving seat and carefully edged one front wheel of the tanker up the left bank, then he quickly jumped back out with his bucket and caught the petrol which came out of the rear port on the right tank.'

"'Yes!" we all shouted when we saw the petrol spurting out. The slope had made all the difference! It was amazing but the driver managed to collect about 2 gallons from that side.'

"'Well in that case, we may as well try the other tank as well," said Wilfred hopefully.'

'The driver smiled at his cheek. *"Aye, we may as well,"* he laughed. *"It's paid for."* With a little gear crunching and careful steering, he managed to manoeuvre the tanker's right front wheel high up onto the opposite bank so as to force any contents to settle behind the rear port on the left tank. This time he was even more successful – there flowed about 3 gallons from that tap and by the time he and Wilfred had carefully poured all the petrol into the little Morris's fuel tank, it was almost full!'

'How we praised the Lord as we set off to further explore the beautiful countryside in the sunshine with the roof open and the gentle breeze flowing through our hair! We were rejoicing all the way home that God had answered Wilfred's prayer so promptly and in such a truly remarkable way. We will never forget our first outing in Wilfred's new car; that we won't!'

Andrew's Gas

Andrew Wommack is the kind of international preacher who oozes faith from every pore.[65] Over the years, he has prayed for and witnessed countless miracles of healing.

However, everyone starts somewhere on their faith journey. When he and his wife, Jamie, began their ministry in a tiny church in Texas, their income was insufficient to meet their needs and Andrew was forced to believe for miracles all the time – just to get by. As he

---

[65] Founder of Andrew Wommack Ministries (1978) and Charis Bible College, Colorado, USA (1994).

freely admits in his inimitable Southern drawl, *"That's not God's best."* Nevertheless, it took Andrew a while to be able to operate in God's blessing rather than having to rely on miracle provisions.

One bleak night, their car wouldn't start and Andrew needed it to be able to get to a meeting at which he was the speaker. Andrew wasn't the best handyman and as he often admits, he wasn't the brightest key in the bunch, but even he soon realised that the fuel tank was empty – the gauge told him so.

ANDREW: *'It was a freezing night and we had run out of gas.'*

'Jamie and I had no spare cash that week, so when the motor wouldn't start, my heart sank. Not knowing what else to do, I decided to lay hands on the car and pray over it in the Name of Jesus. We needed to get to the meeting.'

'I have always been a great advocate of acting on your faith, so now was the time to put my faith into practice. I climbed back into the driver's seat and turned the key; the car spluttered to a start and I shouted, *"Thank you, Jesus!"*'

'I got all the way to the meeting and back with no problem. It was amazing. In fact, over the next few days, I just kept on driving wherever I needed to go. Before getting in, Jamie and I would lay hands on the bonnet and command the motor to start in the Name of Jesus. It was a miracle, but the motor started every time!'

'After that, our car ran for **a whole week**, with an ample injection of God-fuel, until the money came in for a top-up of gasoline in the normal way. Then the miracle stopped.'

'The more I see God do, the more I know it has nothing to do with me. It's not my goodness … it's His!'

CHAPTER 13: God's Cornucopia

'God can do a lot with a little when you offer it to Him.'

Ps. GERARD KEEHAN

Hetty's Oranges

WALTER: *'God is still in the business of amazing us with answered prayer.'*

'Willie Burton, Field Director of the Congo Evangelistic Mission, took his wife, Hetty, with him on an extended preaching tour around the villages in his region. After a few days, Hetty fell ill with malaria and she became so dehydrated that her tongue was sticking to the roof of her mouth. Bearing in mind that they were out in the bush, in a borrowed hut on the outskirts of a native village, without running water or medical supplies, Willie felt helpless to treat his wife's fever.'

'The following day Hetty cried to Willie, *"Oh, if only we had some oranges to suck!"*'

'*"Oranges in the tropical forests of the Congo Basin? - Impossible!"* That's what Willie thought quietly to himself whilst gently mopping Hetty's brow with his handkerchief. Still, he lifted a heartfelt plea to the One for whom nothing is impossible.'

'Meanwhile, a couple of days before Hetty fell ill, the Lord spoke to a missionary across the Congo River, prompting him to send some ripe oranges from their specially cultivated tree at Mulongo to the Burtons. Straight away, he picked his best oranges and placed them in two long baskets. He placed them on the shoulders of two lads from his compound telling them to find Mr. and Mrs. Burton on their Mission Station at Mwanza and to present them with all these lovely oranges!'

'When the carriers arrived at Mwanza, they found that the Burtons were in the villages preaching the Gospel. Not daunted, those two stalwart lads enquired all along the route taken by the Burtons and they eventually found them, with Mrs Burton lying on a camp bed in a hut still crying out for oranges!'

'Willie left the hut when he heard the commotion outside and there to his delight and amazement were the carriers with two baskets full of beautiful oranges. Those oranges not only met Mrs Burton's longing borne from a desperate need for rehydration and the vitamin C to fight her infection but they brought joy to their hearts for God had heard their cry even before it was uttered.'[66]

---

[66] Isaiah 65:24 – 'It shall come to pass That before they call, I will answer; And while they are still speaking, I will hear.'

Dorothy's Provisions

Dorothy Brinkman (née Willis) was born in October 1920. As a trained nurse and midwife, she first met my mother, Hilda, at Willersley Castle near Matlock, Derbyshire where they were both working as midwives during the Second World War. Their lives have followed extraordinarily similar patterns and a long friendship has ensued over six decades. Both were accepted as missionaries to the Congo by the Congo Evangelistic Mission during the 1940s. In later life, Dorothy and my parents attended the same Church in Nottingham for many years and they still visit each other regularly.

Dorothy travelled to Africa alone as a single missionary in 1947 and stayed there for six years during her first term. Her fiancé, Wilfred Brinkman, whom she had met at Bible School, was not able to join her initially but two years later, they were reunited and married. They had two children, Andrew and Faith. I used to sit next to Dorothy's son, Andrew, in the same class at Sakeji Boarding School in what was then Northern Rhodesia (now Zambia).

It was a real life of faith for our missionaries in those days, being totally dependent upon donations from friends and families back at home in England. All the missionaries shared the donations but sometimes there was not enough money to go around. Worse still, at other times, no cheques would arrive from England for months at a time. The only option then was to pray.

The Eggs

DOROTHY: *'In the Congo we had to live by faith.'*

'An extraordinary miracle provision took place shortly after Wilfred and I were married, during my first term in the Congo. At the time, we were not receiving any cheques from England and consequently we were struggling to find enough food to eat. There were two other families at Kashukulu Mission Station where we lived and we were all in the same predicament.'

'I had reared some scrawny chickens, which normally gave me two or three small eggs per week. Things became so dire that Wilfred and I were subsisting almost entirely on these for protein in our diet. Not knowing what else to do, I prayed. That week, my chickens laid twelve eggs instead of three. I was able to give three eggs to each of the other families on the mission station to help them out, and Wilfred and I shared an egg almost every day. It wasn't much but it kept us alive.'

'The chickens continued to produce twelve eggs every week for two months until we received a cheque and were able to afford to buy some food. Immediately our cheque arrived, the chickens returned to laying only two to three eggs per week as before.'

The Flour Sack

DOROTHY: *'God's supply is always there when you need it most.'*

'There were no bakery stores in the Congo when my husband, Wilfred, and I were there in the 1940s and 1950s. During our second term, we lived on a Mission Station called Mwanza, way out in the bush and far from civilization. I had to do all of our own baking, so we were far more dependent upon ingredients such as flour than we are here in England. Once a month, we used to travel the gruelling 160 miles from Mwanza to a town called Kamina over appalling forest tracks to do our shopping in the grocery store there. Can you imagine having to travel 160 miles just to do your grocery shopping? Naturally, our provisions were bought by the sackload and a sack of flour would last us for about three months. Every now and then, missionaries from interior stations such as Ngoimani or Kisanga would pass through and offer to do some shopping for us, which was a great relief if we were running out of certain provisions or we had forgotten to buy something on our last trip.'

'In the dry season of 1954 during our second term in Africa, we went on our usual shopping trip and to our dismay, found that there was no flour available in Kamina. I had only half a sack of flour left at the Mission Station and I was quite concerned as to whether we would manage to last out until the next shopping trip was due. On our return, I continued to bake bread as usual and whenever we had visitors, I would bake a cake in their honour.'

'During that month, no cheque arrived from England, so we were desperately short of money by the time our next shopping trip was due. I checked all our provisions so as to only purchase the most necessary items. It was then that I realised that the sack of flour was still half full, even though I had not been rationing our supplies or baking any less than usual. I called Wilfred to have a look at the sack and he was as amazed as I was. Still, flour was top of my shopping list as we made the difficult journey to Kamina.'

'We were dismayed to find that once again, there was no flour in the whole of Kamina. We had fully expected that there would have been a delivery of flour by then. Our diet depended upon the bread that I baked and, on the way back, we cried out to God for His help. During the second month, I continued to bake as usual, not scrimping in any way, but this time I took much more notice of the contents of the sack. Every now and then, Wilfred would help me to measure the level of the flour in the sack and each time, the level was exactly the same. Throughout the whole of the second month, the flour sack remained half full and we were well fed.'

'At the end of that month, the treasurer of our Mission asked all of the missionaries throughout the entire region to pray because we were all in the same predicament. Not one of us had received a cheque and there was nothing to share out. Wilfred and I were becoming quite concerned. We had a young son to care for and we were running desperately short of many items. Having scraped together every franc that we could muster, we set off for Kamina once more in the hope of buying a few essentials.'

'Imagine our consternation when yet again we found that the expected delivery of flour had still not arrived at the grocery store. We had to face a third month without money and without any fresh supply of flour. Nevertheless, Wilfred and I did not grumble about it.

We just told the Lord and left it with Him. During that month, I continued to bake as usual. By the end of that time I just couldn't believe it. I called my husband and said, *"Can you see the level of the flour? It still hasn't gone down!"'*

'Wilfred checked the level carefully and agreed with me. It was nothing short of a miracle. The sack was still half full of flour, just as it had been three months earlier. During the whole of that time, I had been baking bread and the occasional cake without any constraint. We had eaten our fill despite having no stipend to live on and very few provisions. It was a full three months before there was flour in the shop at Kamina. During all that time, my sack of flour stayed half full.'

'Finally, we received a cheque and the flour delivery arrived in the grocery store. That very week, the flour in my sack went from half full to empty, all in the space of one week, despite the fact that I was just baking as usual, whenever we needed a loaf of bread.

The Tomatoes

DOROTHY: *'God doesn't perform miracles if we don't need them.'*

'On another occasion when Wilfred and I were short of food and out of money, God provided us with tomatoes – gigantic ones!' At the time, our only reliable source of food was a sack of flour for making bread. We also kept a sack of rough salt, which was invaluable for bartering with the natives for some of their food. They would come to us for a measure of salt and offer us, perhaps, sweet corn or bananas from their gardens in exchange. Even so, we were struggling to get by and although we were never hungry, we did not have much variety in our diet.'

'Once again, our only option was to pray. That week the puny tomato plants that I had been nurturing ever so carefully in our little garden plot began to grow vigorously and produce enormous ripe tomatoes. This was so unusual, because in the African heat, and with all the insect pests devouring the leaves, we had only ever managed to produce small, tough-skinned specimens before. This bumper crop came at just the right time, when we needed it most.'

'For at least three weeks, with enough flour to make bread and a prolific supply of tomatoes, all we had to eat for breakfast, lunch and dinner were fried tomatoes on toast! Poor Wilfred! He did complain so, but our little miracle kept us going until the next cheque arrived.'

'We know that this was not just coincidence, but a true provision from God, because no matter how hard we tried after that, using the same care and attention, we never again produced anything but very small tomatoes from our tomato plants in the Congo.'

$$\rightsquigarrow$$

After all those years spent in Africa, very often having to rely on God for the next meal, it is no wonder that Dorothy Brinkman has become a real 'prayer warrior' in her latter years. After all, they say that practice makes perfect. Well, Dorothy has had lots of practice on her knees in prayer and she is an inspiration to all who know her.

I love to hear her pray. She simply talks to the Lord and tells Him her need. Then she leaves the problem in God's hands.'

Wesley's Food Supplies

Wesley and Hannah Beardsmore are my parent's closest life-long friends and missionary colleagues. The account of how God miraculously provided food for them during their house arrest by the Simba rebel army in 1964 is a perfect example of how God is more than able to supply our daily needs, even in the most difficult and dangerous of circumstances.'

WESLEY: *'God used the United Nations to feed us!'*

'In the early part of 1964 just prior to the Simba uprising, I was in the process of completing the long-awaited secondary school building at our Lulimba Mission Station in the Kivu Province of Congo, Africa. My co-missionary, Jim Liddle, was helping me with the building work. We made our own sun-dried bricks for the project, but several times I had to leave him with the African labourers whilst I drove our Land Rover and trailer to the Port of Albertville some 125 miles away on the shores of Lake Tanganyika, to buy bags of cement.'

'On one such occasion, as I walked along the main street in Albertville (now called Kalamie), I saw a tall military figure leaving an office building up ahead. As he glanced back along the street he happened to recognise me, so he waited for me to walk up to him. He was the Swedish commander of the contingent of United Nations soldiers who had been stationed in this strategic town for some time with a view to maintaining a semblance of peace in the volatile political vacuum following Independence from the Belgian colonialists on 30th June 1960. Many tribal factions had been warring to gain power within the various Congo provinces ever since Independence and in our area we were also contending with subversive influences from external power-hungry militia based in neighbouring Rwanda to the east.'

'The commander opened our conversation by telling me that his men were under orders to leave and that he was preparing to do so as quickly as possible. It appeared that the political situation was worsening. He went on to say that he had been mulling over a particular problem and had suddenly seen the solution when he spotted me.'

'His problem — what to do with a large consignment of food supplies for his men that had come up from Dar es Salaam on the coast and had been shipped across Lake Tanganyika from Kigoma to Albertville via the lake steamer? All the boxes had been unloaded from the ship and were stored in wagons on the railway lines at the port.'

'His solution — might he offer it all to the missionaries up-country? He was sorry not to be able to spare any of his soldiers to help, because they were moving out, but if I could manage to unload the trucks, then I could have all the foodstuffs as a gift. Quickly, without going to the merchants for the cement, I hurried back over the Lukuga Bridge and about 5 miles along the road to the small mission compound where Cyril and Barbara Cross were temporarily staying before travelling inland to Makombo mission station. I called Cyril to bring out his Land Rover and trailer, telling him excitedly that we had something other than cement to transport this time!'

'Cyril and I had to make repeated trips to and from the docks to unload all of the railway wagons and take them back to the mission compound. Poor Barbara was beside herself trying to accommodate all the boxes. Then we began the painstaking job of transporting most of the consignment the 125 miles, back and forth up the escarpment to Lulimba. My wife Hannah had not seen such vast quantities of food since leaving England, not even in a shop! It was a veritable cornucopia. But God knew what was just around the corner for us and what we would have to endure in the days that lay ahead. He had sent the provision just at the right time because our lives were precious to Him. The split-second timing had been perfect: if I had not been walking along the main street in Albertville just at the very moment when the Swedish commander left that building, none of this would have happened and we would have starved to death in the coming months.'

'At Lulimba, Jim and I stored the boxes first of all in part of the mission workshops, but then when news reached us that rebel fighters had reached Fizi, the government post on the other side of the mountain range, we had to think quickly where to hide them. The rebels were not called Simbas (lions) for nothing! They would tear us limb from limb to get at such a valuable consignment of food.'

'It so happened that one of our rooms next to the kitchen in the main mission house had no ceiling. This gave us an idea; we had recently purchased a stock of planks for making into school desks and now these could be just what we needed to create a hideaway. We cut the planks to the right length and made a temporary ceiling for this room. Using a ladder, my sons Ralph and Graham helped me and Jim to stack all the food boxes across the entire roof space and then we closed up the entrance to the new ceiling with loose planks. No one would suspect that they were there.'

'Soon after daybreak the next morning, Saturday May 30th 1964, the first group of rebel commandos arrived in a stolen vehicle. They searched the house for guns, ammunition and radio-communication sets; but thankfully never thought to look in the roof space above the ceilings. They commandeered the one visible Land Rover and drove off with our barrels of petrol and many valuable tools and spare parts for the Land Rover such as springs and tyres, which were at a premium in those remote parts of Africa.'

'For some time previous to this, the mission staff at Lulimba had consisted of Hannah and myself, Jim and Naomi Liddle and Kathleen Lucas. With our boys Ralph and Graham and baby Liddle, we numbered 8 persons. However, just 2 days before the Simba rebels arrived, 6 more missionaries had arrived from Makomba mission station loaded up with as much as they could carry in 3 vehicles. They were Cyril and Barbara Cross with their small daughter, Margaret, in their Land Rover; Geoff and Brenda Hawksley in another Land Rover and Audrey Brereton in her small VW car. They had been warned of impending trouble and had decided to temporarily vacate Makombo and take refuge for a time at the small mission in Albertville, which was thought to be a safer place. Unfortunately, by breaking their long journey at Lulimba, they became trapped with us by the sudden arrival of the first wave of rebels.'

'Our totally unexpected windfall of food was certainly going to be needed. We were cut off from all normal food supplies and we didn't even have the petrol to attempt a clandestine escape through the mountains, had we even dared to do so on that first morning. Fortunately, we had the foresight to hide all but one of our vehicles in the bush. If we had hidden them all, the rebels would have suspected something and gone searching for them, but the capture of one Land Rover seemed to satisfy them, at least for the time being.'

'Those first rebel scouts were soon followed by many more groups who took up residence in the Catholic school buildings and government rest camp in Lulimba village itself, about 3 miles away from us. They quickly set up road barriers at the end of the mission drive and across the roads leading out of Lulimba and so then escape was quite impossible.'

'Regarding the large supply of food which we had hidden away: hiding it was one thing, but how to make use of it to feed so many hungry mouths was quite another thing entirely. The Simbas had eyes everywhere. The problem was solved by designating Sunday morning as the most suitable time to retrieve a week's supply. Hannah and Kathleen with our boys Ralph and Graham would stay at home whilst the morning service was in progress and all the local people were in the church building. Kathleen would stroll around outside the kitchen area to keep a lookout for any of our "feathered friends" as we referred to them because of their Red Indian type headdresses. Assuming all was quiet; Graham would gain access via a ladder into the roof space, and carefully hand down boxes to Ralph and his mother. If Kathleen began to sing; they would quickly stop their work, replace the couple of planks they had removed at the edge of the ceiling, stow the ladder away, and wait until Kathleen gave them the all-clear to resume their work again.'

'Each week Hannah divided the retrieved tins of food into 14 piles and distributed these proportionately to each family or group that ate together. The large canteen type cans contained a good variety of foodstuffs such as whole chickens, tuna fish, sliced peaches, tomatoes, jam, spam, corned beef, powdered milk etc. During the 129 days of our captivity these luxury army supplies were supplemented by more basic foods such as rice, maize flour and eggs, which were smuggled in to us by Christians from villages both near and far away. These loving converts risked their lives over and over again to run the gauntlet through rebel lines to bring us any of their own staple food that they could spare. They themselves were struggling to survive since their gardens were continually being raided by rebel soldiers, yet during all that time God protected their lives also and met their various needs. Each of us spent much of our time in prayer during those perilous days. Prayer kept us going and gave us hope, even when in the natural, all hope was gone of ever escaping alive.'

'What seemed to be a very large supply of tinned food at the beginning had almost all gone when at long last we were delivered by Congolese soldiers on October 4th 1964. During those tense days and nights, some of us faced the threat of rape or death many times and all of us were nearly killed on several occasions, but never once were we hungry. God saw to that and He also protected us from pillage, mutilation and death, which in itself is another story …'

Our Frozen Meals

My husband loves to tell how God helped us at a time when we were struggling for money to buy food. It is wonderful that our Father in Heaven cares for even our most basic needs.

MICK: *'We don't have to beg for bread. We're God's children!'*

'My wife, Pearl, used to work as a Technical Author for a submersible pump company in Nottingham. At the time, we were supporting our five children and the mortgage rate in England was sky high at around 15% per annum. Our mortgage repayments had risen by over £300 each month and neither of us were earning sufficiently to cover the heavy demands on our salaries. After paying essential bills, we had only £10 left per week to cover all household expenditures such as food and clothing. I remember that one particular week, the children had been exceptionally hungry at the weekend and there was virtually no food left in the cupboard to last us until my next payday at the end of the week. Pearl and I were distraught and cried out to our Heavenly Father for help.'

'The next morning, as Pearl began to organise the day's work, her assistant nonchalantly asked her, "*Pearl, do you happen to like vegetarian food?*"'

'"*Well, I guess so,*" she replied, not quite sure where the question was leading.'

'"*The thing is,*" he muttered, almost apologetically, "*I've been given a load of ready-made frozen vegetarian meals and I don't know what to do with them because I really hate vegetarian food.*" He lowered his voice as if offering the worst possible gift imaginable. *"I don't suppose you'd like them, would you? I've got a boxful in the car. I was going to ditch them but I thought I'd check with you first just in case you could make use of any of it."*'

'I would love to have been a fly on the wall at that precise moment. I'm sure it took some self-restraint from Pearl to refrain from hugging him with joy! What an answer to our prayer!'

"'I certainly could use them," she exclaimed happily. *"I don't care what they taste like!"'*

'The little man who had been God's instrument to supply us with a freezer full of tasty ready-cooked meals could have had no idea of how timely and important that singular act of kindness was to a struggling family such as ours, at that time. For all he knew, we could have been thriving – wealthy, even. He was only a temp. with no vested interest in helping his provisional boss. He had even been scared that his actions might have offended her. Yet God used him to meet our need!'

'It was such a fabulous week after that. We feasted and dined on the most interesting meals imaginable, all prepared ready for us to heat up and eat. They didn't taste at all bad, either, which I for one was very surprised about. Best of all, we didn't have to go hungry once because God is our Heavenly Father and as King David observed in the Psalms, *"I have never seen His seed begging bread."*[67] We can say this with confidence ourselves now because God has proved His faithfulness to us over the many years that we have been together.'

---

[67] Psalm 37:25

A Bergen Loaf

Don't you just love it when God does something special that says, "*I love you*"? It happened to me during the November snowfalls of 2010. The whole of England was taken by surprise when we were almost brought to a standstill overnight by a sudden cold spell and heavy blizzards. We woke up on the morning of Monday 29th November to find ourselves buried under a thick blanket of snow and it was still falling. Hardly anyone ventured out that day.

The next day, my husband Mick spent 4.5 hours clearing snow off the drive in the vain hope of being able to get to work. He had just finished when the snow started falling heavily again and there was no option but to abandon the idea for another day. Meantime we were running out of essential provisions and with elderly parents to care for, this was becoming quite serious. Mick continued to help digging neighbours out the following day and one kind lady over the road gave us a bottle of milk by way of recompense, which was such a great relief. The family opposite us spent the day creating an enormous igloo with a snowman in front of it. Despite this, their garden was still covered in a thick layer of snow. The snow piles and drifts all around us were about 5ft deep and counting!

On Thursday when we opened the curtains, Mick noticed that a milk delivery lorry had jack-knifed in the hollow at the bottom of our street, totally blocking access to and from the estate. My brave husband took his shovel and even before he had eaten any breakfast, he stoically braved the elements to try to free the lorry. I followed closely behind to see if there was any bread or milk at the local shop, slithering and sliding all the way in the deep, crisp snow.

I had never seen the corner shop so busy! The shelves were being cleared at a phenomenal rate and I ran towards the last two cartons of milk just in time to be able to claim one for myself. What a relief! At least we would be able to make a cup of tea, although a single pint would not last long in our household. I then hurried to the bread counter just in time to claim the last few small cobs (rolls) of bread. All the sliced bread had gone. My neighbour and shared these few cobs between us gratefully - at least these would see us through lunch. The shop manager informed us that he was about to close and he wasn't sure if and when he would be re-opening due to the heavy snow. Supplies simply weren't getting through.

As I made my way gingerly into our street, my ankle boots encased in plastic bin liners to protect my legs from the deep snowdrifts, I noticed that Mick had been joined by an AA man and a couple of council workers who had been sent to clear the blockage made by the milk lorry. An hour or so later, when with their help the lorry had almost backed as far as the roundabout, several of us asked if we could offload the milk and take it to the shop around the corner where he had been trying to make his delivery.

"Oh no!" he said, "The milk is unsaleable now – I've been on the road too long and my boss says that I must return it to the depot in Birmingham."

"Well, couldn't you at least give some to the people who have been helping dig you out of the snow as a goodwill gesture?"

"Oh no, no, no! I can't do that! I have to take it all back."

We were flabbergasted. Hundreds of people in our village would now be without milk or bread and yet here was a lorry-load of fresh milk that had been in a natural refrigerator surrounded by snow and it was all going to be poured away at the depot. What stupidity!

After all that digging, Mick's back was in agony so he returned and lay on our sofa completely tuckered out. I hastened to make him a nice cup of tea and covered him with a blanket to warm his shivering and aching bones.

Half an hour later, Mick started complaining that his tummy felt uncomfortable and that he was feeling sick. I couldn't understand what the cause could be until I checked the date on the small carton of milk that I had just bought at the shop. It was a day past its "Use By" date. What irony! The shop itself was quite happy to sell out-of-date produce, yet the delivery of fresh milk was returned just because the refrigerated lorry had been stuck in the snow for about 3 hours. The remainder of the sour carton of milk would have to be boiled to make it safe to drink.

By the end of the week we were in desperate need of supplies. The snow had not abated and even when the sun did show its face, it was too weak to melt the compacted ice and snow on the ground. Saturday morning, I could see cars skidding down the street, revving wildly and getting into all kinds of scrapes in their effort to escape our snowy prison. One couple, in their panic, locked themselves out of their car as they both tried to push it over an icy ridge. The engine was still revving loudly and they had to borrow a spade to break through a window to gain access. With only a single treacherous, narrow trail down the street and heaps of snow piled high on either side, the road looked like a slalom track. If one car was coming up the street and another was travelling in the other direction, one vehicle would have to give way and back all the way down the street until they could find somewhere to tuck in. The times I witnessed near misses as cars would slide sideways perilously close to slamming into an abandoned car by the side of the road.

It was in this snowy mayhem that I urged Mick to hurry up as he had promised to try to drive me to the supermarket before all the bread and milk had disappeared. When we arrived, the car park was full and Mick had to drop me off and park some distance away. I made a bee-line for the bread aisle. I desperately needed a sliced loaf of brown bread to make Mick's sandwiches for the following week. He had become rather partial to seeded Bergen bread and would often reject any other kind.

"Oh, Lord," I prayed, *"please help there to be a Bergen loaf left for Mick."*

I turned into the bread aisle and gazed in horror at all the empty shelves. All the bread had gone. People were jostling up and down the aisles, their trolleys fighting for space. I scanned each empty tier until I imagined, just for one moment, I could see a single loaf right at the far end on the next to bottom tier.

"Oh, Lord," I pleaded, *"Please save it for me."*

I could see people scanning the empty shelves just as I had done. Several trolleys were coming in the opposite direction. I wanted time to stand still. I needed that loaf!

"Oh, Lord," I panted, *"Please don't let anyone see it."*

I sped down the aisle, past the others who were gazing in disbelief at the empty shelves. Not one person had moved towards my loaf of bread. Somehow, not one other person had spotted it!

"Thank you, Lord! Oh! Thank you, Lord!" I cried as I neared the shelf and recognised the wrapping. The man standing right next to it hadn't even seen the loaf.

I grabbed it, squeezed it, disbelieving that it could be fresh. There had to be something wrong with it that people had passed it by. It was the very last loaf of bread on all of the shelves and God had saved it for me! And … miracle of miracles … it was a Bergen loaf, just as I had asked for!

Tears flooded down my cheeks as I continued to shop. All day, I kept saying, *"Thank you, Lord. Thank you, Lord."* I felt so loved by my Heavenly Father.

CHAPTER 14: Answers to Prayer

'Prayer bends the omnipotence of heaven to your desire.' [68]

Prayer changes things. That's what the Bible shows us through many examples and millions of Christians today are proving this to be true in their everyday lives. It's not rocket science. When you accept Jesus as your Lord and Saviour you suddenly find yourself in the enviable position of having a friend and ally in Heaven[69] who is committed to your welfare and development for the rest of your earthly life and beyond. Because of what Jesus accomplished by dying on a cross to bear the sins of mankind and then rising from the dead to give us victory over sin and death, He has made a way for everyone who believes in Him to become a child of God[70].

Like any father, God loves us dearly and responds when we ask for His help. So, there it is. *'Ask and you will receive,'*[71] Jesus said. The answer may not necessarily be exactly what you asked for

---

[68] The famous Victorian Baptist preacher, widely hailed as the 'Prince of Preachers'.

[69] Romans 8:34 'It is Christ who died, and furthermore is also risen, who is even at the right hand of God, who also makes intercession for us.'

[70] John 1:12 'But as many as received Him, to them He gave the right to become children of God...'

[71] John 16:24 'Until now you have asked nothing in My name. Ask, and you will receive, that your joy may be full.'

or come in the way you expect, but it will always be what God knows is best for you in the long run.

Dad's Forest Guide

WALTER: *'You've got to know God in a very personal way.'*

'In 1945, over sixty years ago, I was going through a forest on my first term in Africa with the best native Christian I had the privilege of knowing at that time, Zaccheasa - a great man of God and a pioneer, indeed. All the villages around us were heathen; there were no churches in those days. We had to start the church from scratch. On this occasion, we had to go across a swathe of forest that was virtually impenetrable. When we got into the middle of it, I could see that Zaccheasa was as lost as I was. It wasn't his territory. Now Zaccheasa knew every tree within 10 miles of his own home. Even in the densest parts he would look around and say in his own language, *"Bwana, we go this way,"* or *"We go that way."* But where we were, 35 miles from his home, he was as lost as I was and so he said, *"Oh Bwana, I don't know what to do, we want Kayika village. I think it might be somewhere over there,"* he pointed vaguely. The trees were so tall, shutting out the sun, that we could get no sense of direction at all.'

'"*Right,*" I said, "*Let's pray.*" We got down with our knees in the soil and we prayed earnestly because we were right in the middle of the notorious Lululwange (Leopard Hill) that was teeming with leopards. These solitary animals used to favour the dense forest as it gave them plenty of cover in which to stalk their prey and rear their cubs. The natives in the surrounding district used to give the Lululwange a wide berth, skirting around its base for the most part. Only intrepid hunters would dare to enter its depths and there were many stories circulating about encounters with the fierce leopards of the Lululwange forest. On one particular occasion, some hunters had wounded a leopard. This animal then stalked them throughout the day. Later on, as they attempted to return home, the leopard pounced on the man who had shot him and mauled him badly as he screamed to his companions for help. The leopard was shot just in time and the injured hunter was then carried by his friends all the way to our Mission Station at Kabondo Dianda where my wife, Hilda, gave him what help she could. The man had 14 deep lacerations across his back where the leopard's claws had penetrated to the bone.'

'It was no wonder that Zaccheasa was as pale under his black skin as I was under my white skin. We prayed and prayed and prayed. We just didn't know what else to do. Then suddenly, Zaccheasa stopped praying and looked up in astonishment for there, in this dense forest, was an African standing beside him, laughing!'

"*Ha! Ha! Ha! Ho! Ho! Ho! .... Na yi ku Kayika* (I'm from Kayika)," the man laughed at the top of his voice.

Here we were on our knees, a white missionary and a black church leader, crying to God to send us somebody to show us the way to Kayika village and this man was a native of the very place we were looking for! God had brought him right there, through impenetrable undergrowth that had no recognisable tracks or paths, to the very spot where we were praying. We didn't realise until we heard the laughter and looked up that God had sent a man right there to help us. We were overjoyed and joined in the merriment until we were all splitting our sides. The man led us all the way into Kayika where I was amazed to find a beautiful village nestled beside a stunning 20-foot-high waterfall. I was even more delighted to find a natural pool at its base where we could bathe away the heat of the day in crystal clear water. It was wonderful to have such a fantastic tale to tell of the day's events at the camp fire meeting that night and it gave us a great opportunity to share our faith in Jesus Christ to the villagers.'

Ryan's Bouncer

Our Senior Pastors at Hope City Church, Sheffield (David and Jenny Gilpin)[72], are a constant source of inspiration both personally and through their inspired preaching. Here are a couple of snippets from the pearls of wisdom that we are treated to week by week:

At one of our Partner's Meetings, David Gilpin told us, *"Miracles happen in impossible situations; it only takes faith"*. He went on to add, *"The first sign of faith is **peace** — we are the **relaxed** partner of the Lord Almighty."*

---

[72] Pearl wrote this chapter in 2009.

Then Jenny stood up and said, *"Faith is always feeling like you're on the verge of something."*

In David's message on the grace of God[73], he stated, *"You can't **try** to believe. Stop it! Jesus said, '**Have** faith in God.'[74] Faith is a "**having**" word, not a "**doing**" word. Once you've got it, you've **got** it. The devil's greatest weapon is to make you think you haven't got faith. But you **own** it. The definition of faith is that you know you've got it before you receive it. There's a divine confidence that comes with faith. You have to dismiss doubt — doubt is a **mental** commodity but faith is a **spiritual** thing. It's okay to be faith-less but not okay to doubt."*

"Don't whip yourself because you haven't heard from God. Don't envy other Christians what they have faith for. You can't embellish faith; either you believe it or you don't believe it."

*"Faith is a little key, not a great roaring giant. Faith transacts with Heaven. It's not faith that opens doors — faith is the little key that opens the door to grace — but it's grace that opens the door to that which God has for you. You don't need **more** faith, you need **less** doubt. You have a key of faith — it may be down the back of the couch but get it out. Right now, you're standing in a field of grace. Stop striving. Grace is right now changing you. You're alive with this stuff."*

---

[73] Delivered on 19/04/09.
[74] Mark 11:22

JENNY: *'Finding faith is not an option in life.'*

'David and I left Australia in 1991 with the divine mandate to 'start a church in every industrial city in the north of England'. So, we began in Sheffield by advertising in the local paper that we were starting a new fellowship and inviting people to come along. Six people turned up that first meeting. I was 4 months pregnant with my son, Ryan, but we were here to build God's Kingdom and God's House, even if it meant lack. This was non-negotiable.'

'David had been unable to secure a job of any kind, mainly because he was too qualified for most jobs. Not even McDonalds would have him, because he was a graduate engineer. With only 5 people regularly attending the church, there was little chance of a stipend there either. In our first house, we had no curtains at our windows and no TV: only a bed and table with chairs and not even a couch to sit on. We had to believe God for dinner every day.'

'But brokenness and faith make best buddies in our lives. Brokenness develops strength within.'

'When I was about to give birth and was the size of a house, David was invited to preach in a church in York. At home, we were still ducking to dress without the privacy of curtains at the windows. There was still only a bed and table with no couch to sit on. Everything we had for the baby was second-hand: his cot, his clothes, pram — everything. We chose to be in that place of lack in order to be where God wanted us to be.'

'That evening, the church in York took up a special love offering for David and me — it came to an astonishing £1,200, which was a lot in 1991! With this gift I was able to furnish my house at last, but only because we had chosen God's Kingdom first.'

'Our son, Ryan, turned out to be a hyper-active child and after a few months, he was driving me wild because he needed constant attention. I prayed desperately to God for a baby bouncer so that I could keep him happily bouncing in one place while I did my work.'

'The next day we sprang a leak in the roof and my husband had to go up into the roof space to investigate. We hadn't been up there before. He searched around and then he found something amazing hidden up in the loft – you guessed it – a baby bouncer! It was the only thing there!'

'Now I don't know if an angel put the bouncer there especially for me or if it had just been left behind by the previous occupants, but it was just what I had prayed for, for Ryan.'

'You've got to find faith in your valleys. You can't allow your valleys to swallow you — you're meant to find springs there. Hold on to God in the lowest ebbs of your life because God wants to transform you. Live for the will of God. It's so worth it. Fix your eyes on what is unseen.'

'After a while in Sheffield, David and I managed to buy a lovely house; however, in 1997, God challenged us to sell our house in order to buy the old warehouse that is now the Mega Centre. We moved into a disgusting old terraced house with paper hanging off the walls that had been there from the beginning. We gave to God even when it hurt.'

'I couldn't buy clothes for the family. In fact, I was 33 before I had a car of my own. But I had come to the painful realisation that the pulpit was God's will for my life, even though I was a painfully shy, retiring person at heart. I had been in ministry for 17 years before I was paid a penny. But the Holy Spirit told me that when God was ready to bless me, I would receive plenty. You need to be willing in the day of battle. You must let persistence do its work and let your life resource many other lives.'

'Now many years later, David and I have a great house overlooking part of Sheffield and wages and cars — but only because we put God's Kingdom first.'[75]

Steve's Neck

Steve Goodhand has been one of our Connect group leaders at Hope City Church and as such, has become a good friend. He is a gentle giant with a very down-to-earth attitude to life that is typical of many a Yorkshire man and he is a constant source of encouragement when it comes to matters of faith. Here is an incident that he shared with us recently from when he was a young man.

---

[75] Matthew 6:33 - 'But seek first the kingdom of God and His righteousness, and all these things shall be added to you.'

STEVE: *'I suddenly felt better.'*

'Just before I became a Christian, I was involved in a car crash that left me with a severe whiplash injury to my neck. I was in absolute agony. I could hardly lift my head off the pillow at times and the pain never left me, day or night. Eventually, a friend of mine called Maggie Bough, whom I knew as a born-again Christian, asked her church to pray for me one Sunday evening.'

'I remember that evening as clearly as if it were yesterday. I was walking along the pavement when suddenly the pain in my neck eased and left me without any explanation. The relief — well, I can hardly explain it. I was able to turn my head, I could breathe easily again and it was no longer an agony to move my shoulders or lift my arms. I couldn't understand what had happened, or why the pain had left me so suddenly.

Out of habit, I looked at my watch and the time was 6.45pm. I made a mental note of it, wondering how long the relief would last. I was half expecting the pain to return at any moment, perhaps even worse than before, but it never did. My family couldn't believe it either, when I told them what had happened.'

'Later on, I happened to tell Maggie about my neck and how the pain had just left suddenly without any explanation. She smiled rather mysteriously and asked me exactly when this had all taken place.'

'"*Last Sunday evening*," I told her, "*I looked at my watch and it was quarter to seven.*"'

'Again, she smiled and nodded knowingly. *"Quarter to seven is exactly when our church started praying for you to be healed,"* she said emphatically. You could see the joy shining out of her eyes as she spoke.'

'That conversation had a huge effect on me, to realise that God could answer prayer so immediately and definitely, without me even knowing that I was being prayed for. Still more profound was the realisation that God was willing to heal the likes of me, who before that time had paid Him little or no attention.'

CHAPTER 15: The Little Things

'Sometimes God answers the shadow of a ghost of a prayer. It's a whisper, a wish, a need.'

MICHAEL EATON[76]

Mrs Pugh

As alluded to earlier in this book, my paternal grandparents, Walter and Lottie Hawkins, pastored a little church in North Wingfield, Derbyshire for many years up until the 1960s. During that time, they gathered a devoted group of members around them, including the Hodson family (*the healing of Alan was described in the 'Friends' Healings' chapter*). The reader may recall that Alan's mother is referred to as Mrs Pugh.

In those days, most folk didn't have a telephone in their homes, so it was impossible to contact friends and family in an emergency. Those who were Christians simply relied on God to help them. Everyone else had to live by their own wits and manage as best as they could.

---

[76] Preacher, writer and scholar (1942-2017)

WALTER: *'Mrs Pugh was devoted to my Mum ever after.'*

'It was 1952, not long after the war ended, at a time when Britain was struggling to recover: money was scarce, food was rationed, many people's lives had been blighted by the war and joy was hard to come by.'

'On this particular day, Mrs Pugh was suddenly faced with a serious personal problem and as a firm believer in the power of prayer, she flung herself on her knees beside her bed and cried to God for help. She poured out her heart before the Lord, sobbing uncontrollably - only He could understand the dilemma she was facing. Very soon, the awful reality of her situation began to weigh more and more heavily on her as the ramifications of her terrible plight unfolded in her mind until finally she was totally overcome with grief and emotion.'

'"*Oh, Lord!*" she gasped, "*I can't take it anymore. Put it on Mrs. Hawkins!*" She sensed that if only God would give my mother an urge to pray for her, then somehow her burden would be lifted.'

'At that very moment, over in Grassmoor, my mother, Lottie Hawkins, had such a tremendous burden come over her for Mrs Pugh that straightaway she stopped what she was doing in the kitchen and went and knelt down by her chair in the living room.'

'"*I don't know what it is, Lord, but something has happened to Mrs Pugh,*" she said out loud. Then she prayed and prayed for much of the day until she felt the burden lift and she knew that God had answered her prayer.'

'At the very moment that my mother **began** to pray, the terrible burden lifted from Mrs Pugh and she got up from her knees, comforted and at peace.'

'That evening, there was a midweek meeting at the North Wingfield Assembly. When Mrs Pugh arrived at the church she could see that my mother was already sitting in her usual seat on the third row back next to the aisle. She walked straight down the aisle and cried out with tears in her eyes, *"Did you get it?"* without even a "hello" or introduction.'

'My mother replied, *"I got it alright and I've carried it all day until I got the victory and felt that the burden had lifted!"*'

Lost and Found

In the parable of 'The Lost Coin'[77], Jesus told a poignant story of a woman who had lost something very precious to her. My RE teacher taught us that in the Middle East in those days, many women used to wear a headband made up of 10 silver coins to signify that they were married, much as we might wear a gold band on our third finger, these days. You can imagine the poor girl's plight if one of her coins had fallen off, leaving an obvious gap in her headband; she

---

[77] Luke 15:8-10

would have been desperate to find the lost coin before her husband noticed that it was missing!

I too have had many experiences throughout my life when I have felt such desperation, having mislaid or lost something precious to me. A couple of weeks ago my daughter, Karen, who is now living in Australia, sent me a beautiful string of fresh water pearls with matching earrings that she had bought when on holiday in Queensland for my birthday present.

It was only the second time that I had worn the pearls. I was tired after a very stressful day in which my mother had fallen, trapping herself in her Zimmer frame and hurting herself rather badly. It had taken all 3 of us - Dad, Mick and I – to extricate her from the frame and lift her up onto the bed. She was badly shaken and bruised, and suffering a lot of pain. Mick was already in bed asleep when I finally crept into the darkened bedroom after trying to settle Mum down but then as I wearily took out the second earring, I heard her calling again for help. I had been trying to poke the stud into its tiny butterfly clip when her shout made me jolt involuntarily and I dropped the clip in my panic. I just had to leave it on the floor or wherever it had fallen and run to my mother's aid.

It proved to be a hard and eventful night. My mother was too weak to get up out of bed and in such agony that I could not even turn her over to change her bedding. The next morning, I had to arrange for a doctor's visit and later had to prepare my mother for admission to hospital, so I forgot all about my earring clip. I accompanied Mum in the ambulance and spent the rest of the day with her on the Admissions Ward. There was no opportunity to eat or even to have a drink except for a small bottle of water that I had thrown into Mum's hospital bag.

By the time I returned home I was shattered. It was only the following morning that I finally began to search on my hands and knees for the tiny gold butterfly clip. It was much smaller than the usual clips found on most fashion earrings, so I knew that I would not be able to substitute a clip from any other of my earrings. It was then that I began to get very concerned when I simply could not find the clip anywhere. I concluded that somehow it must have landed on my clothing when I dropped it and that it could have ended up anywhere in the house.

Over the next few days I continued to search for the clip in between caring for my father, catching up with the housework and visiting my Mum in hospital. I was mystified where the clip could have gone to and very sad because it was a gift from my darling daughter in Australia whom I missed very much indeed. Without the clip, I could not wear the precious pearl set that had cost her so much time and effort and money to purchase for me.

That week we shifted all the bedrooms around in the house and dismantled my father's study so that we could create a downstairs bedroom for my mother when she returned. Everywhere was in chaos and finally I despaired of ever finding the earring clip. Every afternoon was spent at the hospital so time was at a premium, especially as Mum was desperate to come home and we needed to be ready for her.

Stupidly, I had attempted to wash her soiled sponge mattress and it was a nightmare trying to get the sodden thing dry again! I had washed it with great difficulty and lots of disinfectant in the bath upstairs and left it to drain there for as long as possible. Mick said that this quality of sponge would never dry naturally and would go mouldy, so I suggested that we would have to put it in the garden and hope that the wind would speed up the process. Then Mick said that it was no use trying to lift the mattress downstairs – we would leave a soggy trail of water everywhere, so he promptly began to thread the thing out of the bathroom window, breaking the wooden blind in the process. Meantime I had run downstairs in a panic and was below, trying desperately to move all the heavy plant pots out of the way and lay a blanket down in time to catch the huge unwieldy thing as it came crashing down. All I can remember is Mick shouting, "*I can't hold it any longer – it's slipping – it's coming down!*" The next thing I knew, the sodden, spongy mass landed on my head and nearly flattened me!

I can laugh now, especially as contrary to all expectations, I did finally manage to dry the mattress over a period of six days. During that time, I was squeezing it and towel-drying it daily on both sides to extricate as much water as possible. Then when it was almost completely dry, I broke my clothes airer under its weight in my rush to get the mattress out of a sudden squall of rain! It was a real palaver, I can tell you!

The day before Mum was discharged from the hospital, I managed to give the house a thorough clean. By then my Dyson was full and just as I was about to empty the canister into the kitchen bin, I simply threw a little wishful prayer up to God.

'Lord, if the butterfly clip is in the canister, please help me to find it.'

I released the mechanism and watched wistfully as the dirt and dust fell into the bin. Scarcely had my prayer left my lips when I spotted a tiny black object fall onto a piece of paper lodged halfway down the bin. It was amongst lots of other loose bits of grit and dirt that were sliding downwards so I rapidly reached in and felt for the tiny object with my fingertips, hoping upon hope that I could catch it in time before it fell to the bottom amongst all the other rubbish. I longed for it not to be just another piece of grit. Somehow my fingers got there just before the rest of the dirt completely covered my hand and obliterated the item.

Imagine my joy and relief when I felt the shape of the object between my fingers – I could tell even without being able to see the item that I had found my precious gold clip! I held the tiny butterfly clip tight as I extricated it from all the long hairs and grey mass of dust and dirt that had fallen on top of it. Gradually as I continued rubbing, a glint of gold shone out – I had found my earring clip at last! My heart just sang to the Lord in grateful thanks. It was only a tiny little thing, but it meant so much to me that the Lord had taken the trouble to answer my simple prayer.

CHAPTER 16: Benson Idahosa

'Brokenness and faith make best buddies in our lives.' JENNY GILPIN [78]

Dad's Visit to Benin City

In June 1984, my father was on a routine missionary trip to Africa that included visiting the AoG missionaries in Nigeria. He was accompanied by his good friend and fellow Missions Council member, John Emmett, with whom he travelled thousands of miles across Africa to encourage and support the missionaries, helping to solve their problems and preaching in their churches. [79]

During their visit to Benin City, Dad first met Benson Idahosa[80], one of Africa's most celebrated and prolific evangelists.

WALTER: *'Benson Idahosa was a Stephen Jeffreys[81] for Africa.'*

'During June 1984, John Emmett and I were on a missionary trip to Africa and our first stop was in Nigeria where we stayed with Andrew and Jenny Daniels who ran the AoG Bible Institute in Benin

---

[78] Co-Founder and Pastor of Hope City Church, Sheffield. Quote dated 26/04/09
[79] See chapter 'Fuel for Thought'
[80] Popularly referred to as the 'Father of Pentecostalism in Nigeria', Idahosa (1938-1998) founded the denomination Church of God Mission International in 1968.
[81] See chapter 'The Jeffreys Phenomenon'

City. We also met up with our intrepid lady missionary Freda Johnson there.'

'Whilst in Benin City, it had been arranged that we would meet up with the great miracle-working evangelist Benson Idahosa and preach in his massive church. I was tremendously excited to meet the man whom I'd heard so much about. John preached for the Saturday evening service then on the Sunday morning it was my turn to preach. The massive church was packed out; it was a privilege to see so many people worshipping together, all dressed in brightly coloured traditional robes, their hands raised to God and utter joy in their faces. I was sitting next to Benson's wife, Margaret, on the platform and beyond was the choir. I had never seen a choir like it in all of Africa; their harmonies and enthusiasm were awe inspiring.'

'It was a tremendous meeting and my ministry was well accepted. At least 30 people responded to the altar call as I drew my message to a close and invited those who wanted to accept Jesus as their Saviour to come forward. Having preached so often in Africa, I knew the people's hearts and was able to share anecdotes and make my point in a way that everyone understood. I didn't even need an interpreter as most people speak English in Nigeria.'

'After the meeting, John and I spent a while chatting with Benson. I wanted to know more about his ministry and what God was doing through him. It was a fascinating, thrilling conversation. Benson was full of excitement — he had recently been taking a crusade in Kinshasa, the capital of Congo, and there were many mighty miracles taking place when he prayed for the people. He had also been to America and other countries, preaching and praying for the sick. He was delighted that God was using him so mightily.'

'I have just been checking my diary from that visit and recalling Benson's account of some meetings he held in Kinshasa in May 1978. He had been staying with the American missionaries there, Mr & Mrs Dodweit. May Dodweit had organised all the crowds, trying to squeeze as many people into the building as possible and putting all the cripples and other people needing prayer into groups so that Benson could pray for them all. One poor fellow who was merely a bag of bones and unable to walk had been placed carefully on the platform so that he wouldn't be injured in the crush of people seeking prayer. He was in full view of everyone.'

'During the service Benson called to the vast crowd, *"Who believes that Jesus will heal this man?"*'

'There were shouts of affirmation from all around the hall.'

'Benson told me that in that instant, he felt a hot anointing come upon him and he commanded those who really believed to stretch out their hands towards the platform.'

'Immediately Benson strode over to the man, who looked more like a dried-up corpse than a live human being, he was so emaciated.'

'Benson stood in front of the man and shouted, *"In the Name of Jesus!"*'

'That was all he said. The man shot up and ran around the platform, totally healed!'

'Benson gasped with emotion as he told me of the tumult that ensued. He described how the crowd heaved in unison, faith flooding their hearts, when they realised that a miracle had just taken place. There was uproar. People with all manner of diseases rushed to the front, jostling and shouting, all desperate for Benson to touch them. The slower ones — blind, crippled and frail — followed on behind, each just as determined to be healed. Benson began to pray for them, one by one.'

'"*I've never seen the like* ...," Benson told me, "*...**all of them** being healed, one after the other, like a chain reaction.*"'

'I was amazed at Benson's account. I have been present at many healing meetings in my life and have witnessed many powerful miracles, but nothing on that scale. Frequently there are one or two exceptional healings among a group being prayed for, but rarely anything on that scale. I was enthralled. I could just picture Jesus in my mind's eye as Benson spoke, when He healed every disease[82]. I also saw in Benson's eyes the excitement felt by Jesus' disciples when they had been sent out into the villages by Jesus to teach and pray for the sick; they had returned full of joy and amazement that even evil spirits were cast out when they prayed.[83]'

---

[82] Matthew 4:23 'Jesus went about all Galilee … healing all kinds of sickness and all kinds of disease among the people'; Matthew 14:36b: 'And as many as touched it *(the hem of Jesus' garment)* were made perfectly well.'

[83] Luke 10:17-18

'Later on that week, John and I were invited to Benson's home to share a meal on the Thursday with many of the AoG church workers from that region.'

'When we arrived at Benson's house, we were introduced to our fellow guests including Gabriel Oyakhilome, the former General Superintendent of the AoG Churches in Nigeria. Freda Johnson told me that during the 15 years he had been Superintendent, the churches had doubled in both quantity and size in Nigeria. She was working in his territories and had witnessed first-hand the massive multiplication in the work of God, largely through miracle ministries such as Benson Idahosa and even Gabriel himself. God was moving mightily in Nigeria at that time and the church was totally on fire for God.'

'When time came for the meal to be served, I looked around for Benson but couldn't see him at the table.'

"*Where is Benson?*" I asked his wife.

"*Oh, he never eats on Thursdays*," she explained. "*It's his day for fasting and prayer.*"

'I was very disappointed at not being able to spend more time with this precious man of God but also hugely impressed by his dedication to the ministry gift that God had given to him. Jesus himself always set aside time to pray - often all night - and He told his disciples that there are certain issues that can only be dealt with by prayer and fasting. I'm sure that this was the key to Benson Idahosa's powerful healing ministry.'

Postscript: BEN ALLSOP

In closing, it was thought that the reader might like to be briefly brought up-to-date with regards to the Congo Evangelistic Mission and some of the other Derbyshire AoG churches referred to in Pearl's writings (namely: North Wingfield, Bonsall and Alfreton).

With reference to the Mission: the information is sourced from the website of Central African Missions (CAM) International, which is the contemporary name of the work originally founded by Burton and Salter in 1915.[84] The summary of North Wingfield AoG is lengthier than the other two, as the author speaks from family/personal experience, whereas this applies less to Bonsall and more so, Alfreton.

This author also wishes to recount Walter Hawkins Senior's involvement in the pioneering of Holmewood AoG, his own church (now 'Abundant Life Christian Centre').

---

[84] https://caminternational.org.uk/about/our-past/

CAM International

In the hundred plus years of the Mission's operation, the charity has pioneered approximately 5,000 churches in the Democratic Republic of Congo (formerly, the Belgian Congo); some of these churches are the largest in the nation. As the reader recalls the humble conditions the Hawkins family and others faced in the first half of the twentieth century, the biblical phrase: *'Do not despise these small beginnings...'*[85] comes to mind!

As the churches have become more established, inevitably the emphasis of the Mission has changed from one of church-planting and putting in place the necessary administrative structures to training and supporting existing local leaders. Examples of current CAM International projects in the Congo include Bible College work, youth training, media outreach, prison work and medical and practical ministries.[86]

The charity has undergone a few name changes in its time, reflecting the changing nature of the political situation in the Congo. After the Independence in 1972 – which resulting in the country adopting the name 'Zaire', after the Congo River – the charity was styled 'Zaire Evangelistic Mission'. The Congo War of 1996-7 – which resulted in the country re-adopting the name 'Congo' – necessitated another name change. Perhaps judiciously, 'Central African Missions' was

---

[85] Zechariah 4:10
[86] https://caminternational.org.uk/about/our-present/

adopted (in the event of any further name changes to the country), also reflecting the charity's desire to broaden its work beyond the Democratic Republic of Congo into the surrounding African nations. A subtle modification to the name in 2013 (the addition of 'International') was advised in line with developments to UK charity law – though also widening the 'reach' of the Mission beyond Central Africa. The name now very much 'covers all bases', including the African diaspora in the UK!

North Wingfield AoG

In 1996, North Wingfield AoG – by then referred to as North Wingfield Christian Fellowship – amalgamated with the AoG at Clay Cross, a nearby industrial/mining town. This was brought about because the North Wingfield congregation were on the verge of outgrowing the building – whereas Clay Cross AoG possessed a spacious Victorian former Free Methodist Chapel on Market Street, but only had eight members. The North Wingfield premises was sold off for £26,000 that year and has since been converted into residential premises; it last sold in 2020 for £242,000. Interestingly, Pearl and Mick Spencer owned the property for a brief period of time.

Although Scripture is clear that '*the Most High does not dwell in temples made by human hands*'[87], there is an element of sadness in

---

[87] Acts 7:48

the loss of this church building. It was not mentioned in Pearl's recollections: but the Lord actually revealed to Arthur C. Colliss in a dream where to find the capstone for the building (in a stream, close to Mill Farm, Grassmoor) – undeniably, an unusual and significant event! As has been mentioned in this book, the building was one of the first purpose-built Assembly of God churches in Great Britain – so aside from its spiritual value, the church building has some heritage significance.

The amalgamated church in Clay Cross was called 'North East Derbyshire Christian Fellowship' (NEDCF) and was further re-branded as 'Clay Cross Community Church' (C4 Church) in 2017, under the leadership of Pastor Mathew Bollands. This author served as a member of this church from 2013-2020 and married his fiancée, Elisha, here – in the midst of the Covid-19 pandemic! – in August 2020.

Bonsall AoG

The church continues in the former Primitive Methodist Chapel off the village High Street, which was purchased by William Potter, as described in this book. The church now operates under the name 'Village Life Church' and remains in fellowship with the Assemblies of God in Great Britain and Ireland. The author recalls that the church was closely linked with Bonsall Camp, which was owned by the Christian Youth Foundation[88]. The author attended the Summer

Camp for two consecutive years as a teenager – as an intern in 2010 - and testifies to an excellent Christian input provided. Pastor Matthew Quinn of Bonsall AoG – who, at the time of writing, remains the pastor - was very much involved, as were his family. The Christian Youth Summer Camps had been running in Bonsall for 60+ years; most notably, the Christian author, Selwyn Hughes, was sent home from Bonsall Camp as a teenager for bad behaviour, as described in his biography![89] The author wonders if the Camp has since changed hands, as Christianity is not overtly mentioned on its website, although it is clear that some Christian groups still hire out the premises.[90]

Village Life Church remains small, no doubt linked to its very rural/remote surroundings – but according to a 2023 church document on their Charity Commission page[91] – they are *'enjoying mild success in reaching out to the community by means of coffee mornings and Craft Club'*. The church membership is growing, for which they thank God.

Alfreton AoG

The author knows very little about this church – now called Alfreton Christian Centre - having had no first-hand experience of it and there

---

[88] https://en.wikipedia.org/wiki/Bonsall,_Derbyshire
[89] Selwyn Hughes: My Story, Crusade for World Revival (CWR), 2004
[90] https://www.bonsallcamp.com/
[91] https://register-of-charities.charitycommission.gov.uk/charity-search/-/charity-details/1052642/charity-overview

currently being no website or social media page to refer to. The current church premises are modern and purpose-built on Hall Street, near the Tesco Superstore. At the time of writing, Brian and Angela Fox co-pastor the work and have done so since 1993.

Walter Hawkins (Snr.) & the Establishing of Holmewood AoG

Given this author was both converted at Holmewood AoG (now Abundant Life Christian Centre) and currently serves there as Associate Leader, it seems fitting to finish this book with an anecdote relating both the origins of the church and Walter Hawkins Senior, whom we have encountered on multiple occasions in this book. This anecdote was told to me by Betty Smith (1929-2018), concerning her late husband, Pastor (Malcolm) Roy Smith (1924-1990), and is still referred to by people in the church, nearly one hundred years later.

In 1926, Walter Hawkins (Snr.) was knocking on doors in Holmewood (perhaps accompanied by Lottie?), seeking to win villagers to Jesus and the Pentecostal testimony. They happened to knock on the door of Mr. and Mrs. George Smith. Smith was a coal miner – as were the majority of men in the area – and he had two sons, Philip and Roy (a daughter, Heather, would follow three years later). The Smiths were not a church-going family, which was still considered unusual for the time. Their youngest boy, Roy, was two years old and severely afflicted with rickets, such that he had bowed legs. The prognosis was that even if he recovered naturally, he would not be able to walk … or at worse, he would die.

Hawkins talked with the Smiths over the threshold about the Lord Jesus – that on the cross, He purchased salvation for humanity, including forgiveness of sins and healing for diseased bodies. 1926 was the year of the UK General Strike which would have affected the Smiths financially – and, of course, this would be decades before the implementation of the National Health Service[92]. One can imagine the poverty and desperation this family endured … and yet now, the Pentecostals were proclaiming a message that God was *active* and *near* and *willing to display His love and power in acts of divine healing*. It is easy to see how the Smiths … with whatever faith they had in that moment … seized this opportunity. What had they to lose?

Remembering the biblical incident where '*God worked unusual miracles by the hands of Paul, so that even handkerchiefs or aprons were brought from his body to the sick, and the diseases left them and the evil spirits went out of them*')[93], the Hawkins' asked the Smiths to lend them a vest that belonged to little Roy. Although God does not promise to always honour this particular method (the apostle Paul wrote that such miracles were 'extraordinary', even by

---

[92] In 1948, under Clement Attlee's Labour government.
[93] Acts 19:11-12

his standard!) … Jesus did promise to <u>always </u>honour faith (an active trust/belief in God). We trust that the Hawkins' were acting in faith here – perhaps even exercising the gift of faith[94], defined by early Pentecostal writer, Harold Horton, as '*a gift of the Spirit to the saint that he might work miracles, or rather receive them*'.[95] They took one of Roy's vests, prayed over it for a period of time, and then returned it. We do not know exactly what happened when the prayer-soaked vest was placed on little Roy – **but something significantly miraculous must have happened, as the entire Smith family** (including Roy's Uncle and Auntie, Frederick and Emie Kilbourne) **were converted.** As Roy would go on to live another sixty-four years and walk quite ably, one can acknowledge that the Lord did bring about a wonderful miracle of healing for the lad – although, interestingly, his legs would remain bowed for the rest of his life.

The Smiths and the Kilbournes began to attend North Wingfield AoG, convinced of the truth of the Pentecostals' testimony by the occasion of Roy's healing. They would walk from Holmewood to the assembly on Chesterfield Road for a number of years until 1939 – when George Smith decided to start his own meetings in the spare bedroom of the Kilbournes' house at 27 Mornington Road. Apparently, a church split precipitated this move, as the Smiths felt unable to support Walter Hawkins succeeding Wilfred Colliss (mentioned previously in this book) as the pastor of the assembly.

---

[94] 1 Corinthians 12:9
[95] The Gifts of the Spirit, Assemblies of God Publishing House, 1934

This seems somewhat sad, as it was Hawkins' evangelistic zeal and faith in divine healing which was instrumental in the Smiths coming to faith in the first place. The author has been told by others who knew Walter Hawkins that he was a lovely, fatherly sort-of-man with a gentle spirit – but that he was not particularly a strong expositor of the Bible, which is consistent with Alan Hodson's testimony in this book. Although regrettable, believers parting company over irreconcilable differences is nothing new – Paul and Barnabus being a familiar New Testament example[96]. Yet, in the providence of God, even instances like this can led to the furtherance of the gospel – as proven by the *Acts of the Apostles* and the histories of both Holmewood and North Wingfield assemblies. So, the small group of Pentecostals would meet at Mornington Road for a decade – up until the installation of their first church building on Tibshelf Road.

Given the church at this time met in the bedroom of a council-owned terraced house, any musical accompaniment to the meetings was out of the question. No doubt the believers struggled to contain their Pentecostal fullness in the context of the need to not be a nuisance to the neighbours! Pastor Smith knew that the ideal would be to have their own church building – a public space in which local people could come and meet with the risen Saviour, Jesus Christ. On the 7th April 1948, George Smith and a group of men from the assembly (Harry Mellows, George Banks, Frederick Kilbourne and Walter

---

[96] Acts 15:36-41

Cooper) joint-purchased land off Tibshelf Road, with the intention of having a church building erected there. The difficulty with this (aside from the financial implications) was that building works were put on hold, as the Second World War had not long since finished. Consequently, a purpose-build church building was out of the question: a temporary, existing structure was needed that could be transported on site. Smith heard about a doctor's surgery building that was for sale in nearby Doe Lea. The following is an extract from Roy's diary (Saturday 15th January 1949):-

'Dad and I went up to the building to see roughly how many we shall be able to seat. We were a bit disappointed (approximately 90).'

This indicates that there was a good deal of faith – even in these early days - for the Lord to raise up a mighty assembly in Holmewood. Despite being a seemingly insignificant 'home group', Pastor Smith had vision for much more. Although the building was smaller than anticipated, the believers bought it and had it transported onto Tibshelf Road. This faithful band then set about making this modest building their sanctuary, using whatever skills they had amongst them to 'get the job done'. Frederick Kilbourne was a foreman on the roads and had the building peddle-dashed; others worked on hand painting the '*Holmewood Assembly of God*' sign which would hang over the porch, as well as the window frames and front door. A *Notice of Passing of Plans* document issued by Chesterfield Rural District Council in 1948 records that the roof of the assembly was constructed principally from '*felt on boards*' and the external walls from '*timber boarding*' – hardly the most robust of buildings! Indeed, the document stipulated that the '*temporary church*' could stand for ten years, after which it should be demolished or an extension period applied for.

We know from Roy's diary that work on the interior of the church building began on Friday 15th April 1949 and finished on Monday 16th May of that year. Although small, the hall was well-heated and particularly comfortable, as tip-up cinema seats were installed rather than conventional pews. The last meeting at 27 Mornington Road took place on Tuesday 24th May and the grand opening of the church building took place the following Saturday on the 28th.

As the photographs indicate, the opening of Holmewood AoG was well-supported by the village and other local assemblies. The building was dedicated to the Lord's service by Pastor Frank Horner, minister of Glad Tidings, Chatsworth Road[97] from 1942-1946. Horner had previously been dispatched by AoG GB to investigate the 16-20 people that met in the bedroom, in response to Pastor Smith applying to the Midlands District Council of the Assemblies of God in 1945 to enquire if their meetings could be affiliated with the Fellowship. Horner had found no fault with what he witnessed and he recommended the group to the General Council for

---

[97] Referred to earlier in this book by its later names: Zion Assembly of God and currently, Lifehouse Church.

accreditation, which was forthcoming with a Certificate of Fellowship, signed by Donald Gee (Chairman) and John Carter (Secretary).

The Opening of Holmewood AoG on Tibshelf Road, Saturday 28th May 1949.

In terms of the church building opening, this short entry in Roy's diary from that day captures the sense of relief and excitement felt by the church as they finally had their own building:

'Opened the new church hall today. Sister Mason turned the key. This is the day we have waited for years for!'

As mentioned previously, Chesterfield Rural District Council had given the temporary church building a ten-year lifespan in 1948. In November 1959, Church Council member E. Cox proposed that *'an architect be contacted to assess the life of the present building and draw up a proposal sketch of a new building (within a budget of £4000)'*[98].

Pastor George Smith, hand stretched out to heaven in prayer. Sister Mason is right of him on the picture with Pastor Frank Horner grasping the door handle.

The members contributed generously to the building fund over a number of years, eventually allowing the erection of the present

---

[98] Quotation taken from the first Church Council Minute Book of Holmewood AoG

building which was opened on Saturday 17th September 1966, debt-free. This building was much larger, modern and obviously purpose-built, complete with a balcony overlooking the sanctuary and a platform, where the pulpit and baptistry was located. Behind the platform (in what would become known as '*the L-shape*'), there was originally a vestry, toilet, kitchen – and beyond that, the boiler house. The new church building was built in front of the former building, which would eventually be demolished in the late 1970s/early 1980s to allow the building of a church hall behind the sanctuary, where the saints could fellowship after meetings.

Unfortunately, Pastor Smith – the man God raised up to establish the Pentecostal work in Holmewood – did not live to see the new building opened. His health began to deteriorate early 1966, necessitating Roy becoming Co-Pastor with him, to ease the burden of ministry on his father. Roy continued his role as Youth Leader in addition to his pastoral responsibilities but Brian Hodson (son of Alan and grandson of Mrs. Pugh) was appointed as Assistant Youth Leader, with a view to eventually taking over the youth work.

Pastor George Smith died on Monday 11th July 1966 – nine weeks and four days before the new church building was declared open. Prior to the official opening, Pastor Roy Smith was formally inducted as minister of Holmewood AoG on Sunday 20th August 1966 in a meeting convened by Les Botham and with District Council representation. At the September official opening, Mrs.

George Smith turned the key of the new church building *(Sister Mason, who opened the first church building, also died in 1966 – and thus the family commissioned a table in her memory on which the Breaking of Bread was celebrated at the assembly for many years)*. George Jeffreys Williamson, who would go on to briefly become Principal of AoG's Bible College at Kenley, Surrey between 1970-71, preached at the 14:20 opening service and the Derbyshire Times provided a write-up of the happy day.

Today, the church is led by Les and Elizabeth Roe (Senior Leaders) and this author, ably supported by a Church Council and Department Leaders. Abundant Life Christian Centre seeks to embody the values of *'Evangelical, Pentecostal, Missional, Inclusive* and *Pioneering'* and, in addition to its regular church meetings, endeavours to remain at the heart of the local community through a range of outreaches including a food bank (Living Hope), charity shop, parent and toddler group (Little Munchkins) and youth group (Dynamite Club).

May our God of *'burning, cleansing flame'*[99] continue to bless the churches and ministries described above – at home and abroad – with 'Showers of Pentecost': that men, women and children *of our day* would come to know the saving grace of God through our Lord Jesus Christ.

---

[99] The Song Book of The Salvation Army #203, General William Booth (1829-1912)

Abundant Life Christian Centre, Sunday 4th February 2024, marking the Centennial Celebration of AoG GB (1924-2024).

Ben Allsop

June 2024

Printed in Great Britain
by Amazon